Economics HL

FOR THE IB DIPLOMA

George Graves

PEAK

Published by:
Peak Study Resources Ltd
1 & 3 Kings Meadow
Oxford OX2 0DP
UK

www.peakib.com

Economics HL: Study & Revision Guide for the IB Diploma

ISBN 978-1-913433-31-4

© George Graves 2021

George Graves has asserted his right under the Copyright, Design and Patents Act 1988 to be identified as the author of this work.

Peak Study & Revision Guides for the IB Diploma have been developed independently of the International Baccalaureate Organization (IBO). 'International Baccalaureate' and 'IB' are registered trademarks of the IBO.

Books may be ordered directly from the publisher (see www.peakib.com) and through online or local booksellers. For enquiries regarding titles, availability or retailers, please email books@peakib.com or use the form at www.peakib.com/contact.

Printed and bound by Severn, Gloucester, a carbon neutral printer on responsibly sourced paper

The purpose of this guide is to assist students with their preparation for the final IB Economics exam. It is not a textbook and should be used in conjunction with all the other sources that the student has. It will aim to identify the main components of the syllabus and present them in a way that will be useful for answering exam questions. Emphasis will thus be given to providing clear and concise definitions, appropriate diagrams and real-world examples that are a major requirement for the new syllabus. I have purposely avoided detailed examination of descriptive topics that can be easily learned from other sources, and have instead concentrated on the underlying theory and concepts necessary for analysing and discussing topics. I also credit the reader with some knowledge of economics and assume a basic level of understanding.

The new syllabus for first examination in 2022 introduced some new material and removed some topics from the old syllabus (2013–21). For example, 'nudge theory' has been introduced and cross price elasticity of demand has been removed. The major changes, however, are with respect to the emphasis on certain economic concepts and the style of the questions that will be asked.

Although this guide will present the topics in the order of the syllabus units and headings, they should not be seen as separate topics but as a logical sequence that is linked together and wherever possible these links and relationships will be identified and discussed. Some of these links are possibly a bit advanced and will be presented in highlighted sections and are intended for the students who like to think 'outside the box' and who are chasing the elusive 7.

You will find a short section showing examples of numerical questions, however there are much more extensive guides produced separately that provide questions and answers for each of the exam papers. I have also written a further guide dedicated to the Internal Assessment.

This guide concentrates on those parts of the syllabus that are most likely to be asked on exam questions. There will therefore not be any attention given to the history of economic thought and the methodology of economic research that have been introduced in the new syllabus. These topics are interesting but are of little practical relevance for exam revision and can be reviewed from your textbooks.

Finally, as do most students and teachers, I will ignore possible links between economic theory and theory of knowledge. The more astute students who are properly taught to apply theory of knowledge will be able to work out the connections themselves.

George Graves

Contents

About this guide

This book is not intended as a substitute for your textbook, class work or independent research; it is more of an additional, focused guide that takes you through the key parts of each topic, provides advice and pointers to other resources or linked parts of the syllabus, and is especially useful for exam preparation.

It is divided into chapters mirroring the structure of the syllabus, with an emphasis on revision questions and answers rather than detailed content. The examples and case studies that are used throughout the book should be further developed with your own research.

You are strongly encouraged to make this book your own: highlight key words or concepts, put your notes in the margin, mark up diagrams, add your own links to other sources, and so on. As well as helping to consolidate your understanding of each topic, this will give a solid base when it comes to preparing for final exams.

Navigating the guide

This guide is structured to enable you to study efficiently:

- topics are covered in syllabus order,
- content is focused on the most important concepts, terms, and information,
- additional commentary is separated into highlighted sections,
- exam tips and example questions accompany the relevant text.

We use icons to help you quickly and easily identify different types of information.

Key to icons used in this study guide

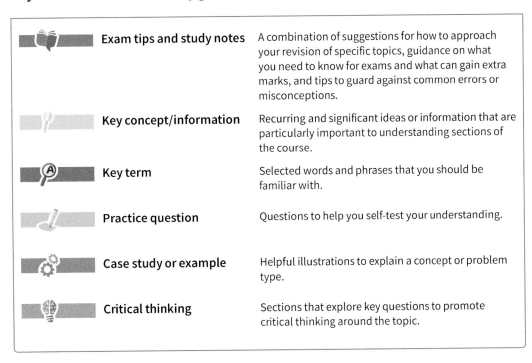

	Exam tips and study notes	A combination of suggestions for how to approach your revision of specific topics, guidance on what you need to know for exams and what can gain extra marks, and tips to guard against common errors or misconceptions.
	Key concept/information	Recurring and significant ideas or information that are particularly important to understanding sections of the course.
	Key term	Selected words and phrases that you should be familiar with.
	Practice question	Questions to help you self-test your understanding.
	Case study or example	Helpful illustrations to explain a concept or problem type.
	Critical thinking	Sections that explore key questions to promote critical thinking around the topic.

Chapter 1: Introduction to Economics

1.1 Key Concepts

There are nine key concepts that you are expected to know and be able to apply, and in fact three of these have to be used as a lens through which you are required to conduct your IA commentaries.

▶ **Scarcity**: this is the most fundamental of all economic concepts and is the very reason that the study of economics exists. It refers to the universally-observed situation faced by all economies of **unlimited wants** on the one hand and **limited means** of providing for these wants on the other.

▶ **Choice**: this is directly linked to scarcity because if it is not possible to have everything that people want to have it is necessary that choices have to be made. The most important are **what**, **how**, **in what quantities**, and **for whom** to produce. It is in fact these choices and the way in which they are made that constitute the main subject matter of economics. A related concept that is observed throughout economics is **opportunity cost** which is the cost of any choice expressed in terms of the next best alternative that is foregone.

▶ **Sustainability**: this refers to the ability of current generations to satisfy their wants without reducing the ability of future generations to do likewise. As a concept it is usually applied to aspects of growth and development and is closely linked to the choices that are made in the face of scarcity. For example, the choices between the use of renewable energy (sustainable) and non-renewable energy (unsustainable).

▶ **Efficiency**: this is a broad concept with several applications and is related to the results of the choices that are made with respect to the best possible use of the scarce factors of production. This aspect is referred to as allocative efficiency and is achieved when consumers pay the exact opportunity cost of producing the product so that the price paid is equal to the marginal cost **(P=MC).** Another aspect refers to the efficiency with which the factors of production are combined, referred to as productive efficiency, and is achieved when firms produce at the lowest level of their average cost. A more general aspect is dynamic efficiency which refers to the effect that different market structures might have on promoting research and development **(R&D)** that leads to innovation and dynamic economic growth.

▶ **Equity**: not to be confused with equality with respect to the distribution of income. The amount of equality or inequality of income distribution is measurable and can be expressed statistically **(positive economics)**, but whether it is equitable involves a value judgment regarding fairness and is therefore an example of **normative economics**.

▶ Economic well-being: this concept has many dimensions that make it difficult to define precisely and again involves value judgements when applying it. It includes feelings of security regarding present and future income, environmental sustainability, empowerment, freedom of expression and equality of opportunity together with several other factors that contribute to the quality of life.

▶ Intervention: as an economic concept it refers mainly to government intervention with the aim of achieving various policy objectives. Such interventions will be observed in all areas of the economy and evaluating them will be a popular type of question on the exam for both paper 1 and paper 2.

▶ Interdependence: this is an important feature of the global economy and has a direct impact on international trade. What happens in one country will affect what happens in other countries through trade links. There are also several other areas of interdependence since all economic relationships and transactions are to some extent linked. The Covid-19 pandemic is a good example of interdependence and how it operates.

▶ Change: this is an essential feature of any dynamic economy because economic activity is an ongoing rather than a static process. For the exam you will be required to identify changes, measure them and assess their impact on the economy.

Nudge Theory

In addition to the key concepts the new syllabus has introduced a relatively new feature of the growing trend towards behavioural theories in economics. The principle of nudge theory is that market behavior can be influenced in subtle ways while retaining the freedom of choice in the market. For example, in 2018 the UK government announced that it intended to introduce a tax on drinks that contained more than a certain percentage sugar content. This motivated some companies to limit the amount of sugar in their drinks. The government could have banned drinks with a high sugar content, but nudging firms towards this result is seen as being fairer than forcing them. Companies have also used nudges as marketing techniques, for example placing sweets at child height level at supermarket check-out counters or restaurants placing the most profitable wine in second place on the wine list. It is not very likely that there will be specific nudge theory questions on the exam, but some relevant real-world examples could enhance the quality of any answer.

Chapter 2: The Fundamental Economic Problem

Economics is a social science that studies how scarce resources are allocated between alternative uses. These scarce resources are described as factors of production which are:

▶ Land

▶ Labour

▶ Capital

▶ Entrepreneurship

These four factors are combined for the production of goods and services but there is a limit to how much can be produced so choices have to be made.

If resources were unlimited there would be no scarcity and no need to make choices.

For any economy the amount that can be produced is determined by the **quantity** and **quality** (efficiency) of the available factors of production. The maximum amount that can be produced is shown by a **Production Possibility Curve (PPC)** as shown in Figure 2.1.

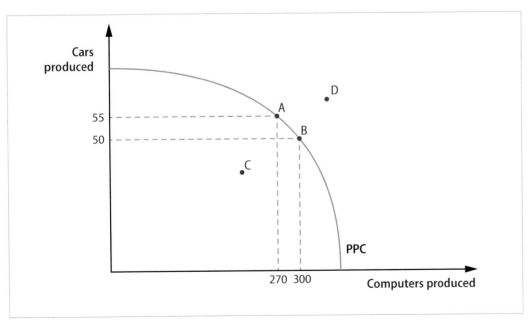

Figure 2.1: **Production possibility curve**

In Macroeconomics the equivalent to a shift in the PPC is a shift in the Long Run Aggregate Supply (LRAS).

The PPC in Figure 2.1 presents a simplified version of the production choices faced by an economy by assuming the ability to use its resources to produce combinations of two goods, in this case cars and computers. Producing at any point on the PPC is possible and means that all resources are fully employed, e.g. at point A or B. Producing within the PPC, e.g. at point C, is also possible but it means that some resources are not being fully employed. Producing at point D is currently not possible but might be achieved in the future by shifting the PPC outwards to the right. This could be the result of an increase in either the quantity or quality of any of the factors of production and is described as **economic growth**.

If the economy is currently producing at point A and wants to have 30 more computers it can only achieve this by sacrificing 5 cars. Moving from point A to point B thus involves an **opportunity cost** of 5 cars for the additional 30 computers. Moving from point C to A or B, however, does not involve an opportunity cost since no current production is being sacrificed.

Chapter 3: Market Equilibrium and Resource Allocation

The economic choices that are necessitated by scarcity can be made either through the free market (price) mechanism or via a central planning agency (government), or as is usually the case a mixture of the two (mixed economy).

The model that is used for economic analysis is the free market economy with various examples of government intervention, i.e. a mixed economy based on free market principles.

A **market** exists whenever there is interaction between a willing **seller (producer)** and a willing **buyer (consumer)**.

The behaviour of producers is described as **supply** and that of consumers **demand**.

3.1 Demand

Consumer demand is the quantity of a product that consumers are able and willing to buy at a particular price in a given time period

The law of demand states that the quantity demanded will be inversely related to the price of the product and with two theoretical exceptions this law is considered to be universal and is illustrated in Figure 3.1.

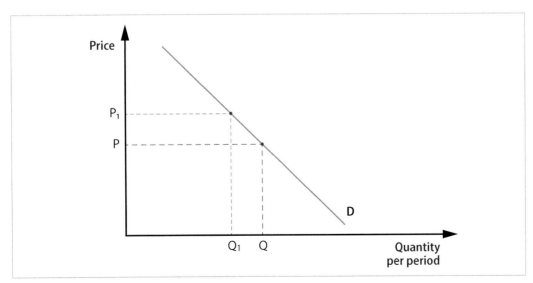

Figure 3.1: **Graph showing demand (D) as a function of price and quantity**

In the case of the law of demand the other things are the **conditions of demand** which determine the actual position of the demand function. Any change in the following will cause the demand to shift:

Here it is appropriate to introduce the assumption *ceteris paribus* or 'other things being equal'. Whenever we want to highlight a specific relationship between two variables we should apply this assumption because other factors could change and affect the relationship.

1. **Income**: this is probably the most important non-price factor that influences demand because it directly impacts the **ability** of the consumer to pay. For **'normal'** goods income and demand will be positively related but there is a category of goods known as **'inferior'** goods for which the opposite applies. Inferior goods are lower priced and less desirable substitutes for normal goods. For example, in many economies basic food products such as rice, potatoes or polenta might be inferior goods to meat, fish and cheese.

2. **Tastes and preferences**: these are influenced by a variety of factors such as fashion, advertising, peer pressure, laws and natural phenomena or events. The recent pandemic has had a significant effect on consumer's spending habits such as the increased demand for masks and hand sanitisers and the increased demand for online platforms such as zoom. Parallel to these changes are the decreased demand for air travel and cruises.

3. **The prices of other products**: some products are in competitive demand (**substitutes**) such as Netflix and Amazon Prime or burgers and pizza, so that an increase in the price of one will cause an increase in the demand for the other. Other products might be in joint demand (**complements**) such as cars and petrol (gas) or cinema tickets and popcorn so that an increase in the price of one will cause a decrease in the demand for the other.

4. **Size and distribution of the population**: more people in total or in a particular age group will influence the demand for certain products e.g. an increase in the birth rate will lead to an increase in the demand for prams and ear plugs.

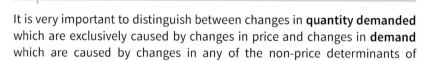

It is very important to distinguish between changes in **quantity demanded** which are exclusively caused by changes in price and changes in **demand** which are caused by changes in any of the non-price determinants of demand.

3.2 Supply

Supply is the quantity of a product that producers are able and willing to produce and sell at a particular price in a given time period. Supply and price will normally be positively related because at a higher price it is more profitable for producers to increase quantity supplied. This relationship is shown in Figure 3.2.

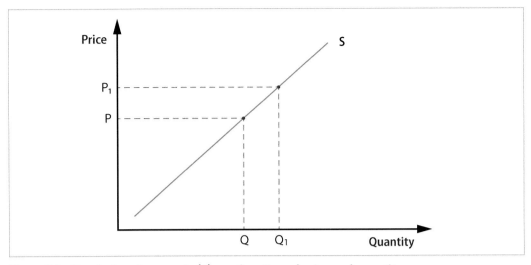

Figure 3.2: **Graph showing supply (S) as a function of price and quantity**

When price increases from P to P_1 quantity supplied increases from Q to Q_1. As with demand there are non-price determinants of supply which determine the position of supply. A change in any of the following will cause the entire supply to shift:

1. **Costs of Production:** this is the most important non-price determinant of supply as it has a direct impact on profitability. A decrease in costs of production will increase profitability and cause supply to shift to the right (increase) and vice versa.

2. **Technological advances:** these will make production easier and are likely to decrease costs of production as for point 1.

3. **Indirect taxes and subsidies:** these affect costs of production. Taxes increase costs while subsidies decrease costs with results as in point 1.

4. **Natural phenomena:** the production of some goods such as agricultural products is influenced by climatic conditions, plant diseases or attacks by insects which can have an effect on actual supply. A recent example is the plague of locusts that devastated food crops in Kenya.

5. **Changes in relative profitability:** price changes of other goods can affect relative profitability and cause supply to shift. For example, if the price of wheat increases, farmers will decrease the supply of barley or corn as they switch to more wheat production. These products are in **competitive supply**.

As with demand it is necessary to clearly distinguish between movements along supply in response to changes in price and shifts in supply resulting from changes in any of the non-price determinants of supply.

Also, when expressing the supply relationship with price it is necessary to make the *ceteris paribus* assumption.

A note on terminology

It is important to express changes in demand and supply with the correct terminology. Any changes resulting from price changes are described as *changes in quantity demanded or supplied* whereas changes resulting from changes in non-price determinants are described as *changes in demand or supply*.

3.3 How demand and supply interact to establish market equilibrium

Market equilibrium is established through the interaction of consumers and producers in the market, each pursuing their own self-interest. Consumers are assumed to aim to maximise their satisfaction (utility) from consumption, while producers are assumed to aim to achieve maximum profit from production. By bringing our concepts of supply and demand together in Figure 3.3 we can see how the equilibrium price and quantity are established in a free market.

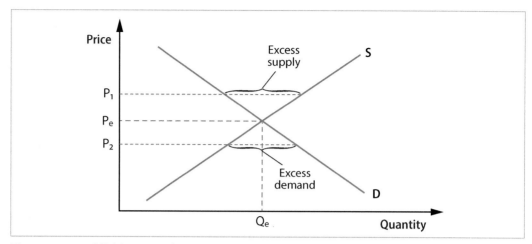

Figure 3.3: **Establishing a market equilibrium**

In a free market there will always be an automatic mechanism that moves the price towards the equilibrium at P_e in Figure 3.3 and at this price the market will clear so that the quantity demanded exactly equals the quantity supplied at Q_e. If price were above Pe at P_1 there would be excess supply in the market that would exert pressure for price to fall, while if the price was below P_e at P_2 there would be excess demand in the market that would create pressure for price to rise.

Once the equilibrium price has been established in a market there will be no pressure for it to change unless there is a change in either the conditions of demand or supply.

The following examples show how such changes lead to a reallocation of resources in the economy and should be used to illustrate the **signalling** and **incentive** functions of the **price mechanism**.

CHANGES IN SUPPLY AND DEMAND

Example 1. Assume an increase in the demand for face masks

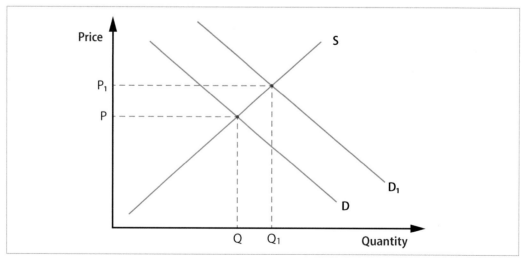

Figure 3.4: **Graph illustrating change in demand**

As occurred during the Covid-19 pandemic there was a large increase in the demand for face masks, indicated by the shift in demand from D to D_1. The result of this was to cause the price of face masks to increase from P to P_1. This created a price **signal** to suppliers that it was now more profitable to produce face masks and they had an **incentive** to increase the supply. As a result the supply of face masks increases to Q_1 and a new market equilibrium is established at a higher price and quantity.

Example 2. Assume a decrease in the supply of cars

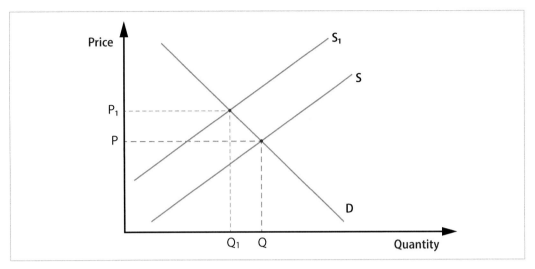

Figure 3.5: **Graph illustrating change in supply**

The pandemic led to many supply chain problems for firms, one of which was a shortage of microprocessor chips that are necessary for the production of cars. As a result, the supply of new cars decreased from S to S_1. This caused the price of new cars to increase from P to P_1 and again this created a price **signal** to consumers who had an **incentive** to decrease the quantity demanded from Q to Q_1.

These types of examples should be used to illustrate how the **price mechanism** operates to **allocate scarce resources in the economy**.

A note on first round and second round effects and simplification of analysis

In the above examples the process of resource allocation has been simplified by assuming that the changes occur quickly and smoothly. In the real-world these transitions are never as quick and may take time going through several stages until the new equilibrium is achieved. (See section on elasticity.)

In addition there will be second round effects on other markets. For example, the decrease in the supply of new cars and large increase in price has led to an increase in the demand for second hand cars. Consequently, second hand car prices in the USA have increased significantly and many car owners have been induced to sell their cars.

Chapter 4:   Elasticity of Demand and Supply

4.1   Price elasticity of demand (PED)

This is a measure of the responsiveness of quantity demanded to a change in price. A numerical value can be calculated as follows:

$$PED = \frac{\% \text{ Change in } Q_d}{\% \text{ Change in Price}}$$

For PED the sign will always be negative because price and Q_d will always change inversely, as stated by the law of demand. For practical purposes however, we ignore the sign and concentrate on the size of the numerical value. The larger the numerical value, the more responsive quantity demanded is to a given price change.

Demand is described as follows:

PED > 1	Elastic
PED < 1	Inelastic
PED = 1	Unit elastic
PED = 0	Perfectly inelastic
PED = ∞	Perfectly elastic

PED can never be perfectly inelastic; as an example, anybody who thinks that the demand for a lifesaving drug is perfectly inelastic is failing to recognise that demand refers to both willingness and *ability* to buy, not just willingness.

4.1.1   PED and Linear Demand Functions

A linear (straight line) demand has the same slope throughout and this is a potential source of confusion because the slope of the demand function is often *mistakenly* thought to be an indication of elasticity. All downward sloping linear demand functions will have varying elasticity throughout their length in the sequence indicated in Figure 4.1.

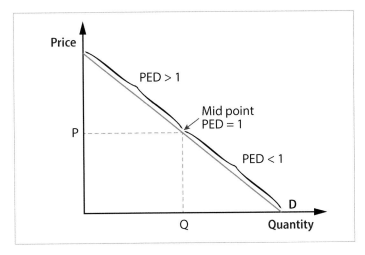

Figure 4.1: **Price elasticity of demand along a linear demand function**

At the mid-point demand will always be unit elastic (PED = 1). Below this point it will be inelastic and above this point it will be elastic.

There are only 3 theoretically possible demand functions that can have the same elasticity throughout as shown in Figure 4.2.

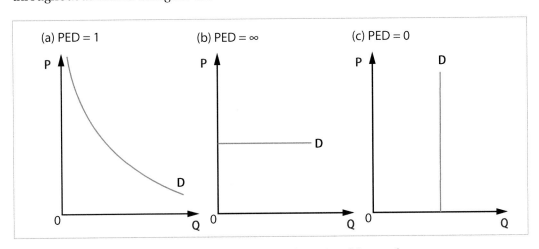

Figure 4.2: **Demand functions with constant price elasticity of demand**

4.1.2 PED and Total Revenue (TR)

Given TR = P × Q

→ PED will determine the effect of any price change on TR

The possible relationships are summarised as follows:

increase in price → *increase* in TR	demand is **inelastic**
decrease in price → *decrease* in TR	demand is **inelastic**
increase in price → *decrease* in TR	demand is **elastic**
decrease in price → *increase* in TR	demand is **elastic**
any change in price → *same* TR	demand is of **unit** elasticity

4.1.3 Factors that influence PED

▶ **The number and availability of close substitutes**: the more close substitutes for a product, the easier it is for consumers to adjust their spending following a price change and therefore demand will be more elastic.

▶ **The proportion of income spent on the product**: the smaller this is, the less elastic the demand. For example, a change in the price of salt or toothpicks is not likely to have any significant effect on quantity demanded as it will have a minimal impact on the average household's budget.

▶ **Time**: consumers can generally adjust their spending quite quickly in response to price changes but the response is not likely to be immediate. It will take some time to find and try potential substitutes and PED will increase over time.

▶ **Luxuries and necessities**: luxuries are said to have a more elastic demand than necessities, at least according to accepted wisdom in the teaching of IB economics.

Determining the PED for a product can be tricky as there might be contradictory factors involved such as many substitutes but a small proportion of income spent on it. The demand for primary products (commodities) is considered to be less elastic than the demand for manufactured goods. If this is the case, is it because of the availability of substitutes, the proportion of income spent on them or the claim that they are necessities whereas manufactured goods are luxuries? Fortunately the IB is quite flexible as long as a plausible examples and reasons are provided.

Luxury or necessity?

I personally find it impossible to provide an objective definition of what constitutes a luxury or a necessity and therefore the distinction is not very useful in the context of PED. Would a 10% increase in the price of diamonds or caviar lead to a more than 10% decrease in quantity demanded? If not does this mean that diamonds and caviar are a necessity?

4.2 Income elasticity of demand (YED)

YED is a measure of the responsiveness of demand to a change in income. A numerical value is calculated as follows:

$$\text{YED} = \frac{\%\ \text{Change in } Q_s}{\%\ \text{Change in Price}}$$

If the good is **normal** the sign will be positive but if the good is **inferior** the sign will be negative. In developed countries basic foods such as bread or potatoes are likely to be inferior goods meaning that as incomes increase the demand for these products tends to fall while the demand for more expensive food substitutes increases. During the global recession following the 2008 financial crisis, falling incomes led to an increase in the demand for cheap fast food products and a decrease in the demand for more expensive restaurants in many countries.

The actual responsiveness of demand to changes in income will be indicated by the numerical value for YED. As with all elasticity concepts: $> 1 \rightarrow$ elastic, $< 1 \rightarrow$ inelastic, and $= 1 \rightarrow$ unit elastic. As tastes and preferences and economic situations change over time it is possible that the relationship between demand and income will also change and what used to be a normal good can become an inferior good. Fifty years ago a bicycle was a normal good in China but now it has become an inferior good as more and more people are now able to buy cars as their incomes have increased.

4.3 Price elasticity of supply (PES)

PES measures the responsiveness of quantity supplied to a change in price:

$$PES = \frac{\% \text{ Change in } Q_d}{\% \text{ Change in Income}}$$

The sign will always be positive since price and quantity supplied will always change in the same direction and the numerical value will indicate the degree of responsiveness of supply to any price change: $> 1 \rightarrow$ elastic, $< 1 \rightarrow$ inelastic, and $= 1 \rightarrow$ unit elastic.

Since supply and price are positively related the slope of the supply function is an indication of elasticity as well as the intercept of the supply function as shown in Figure 4.3.

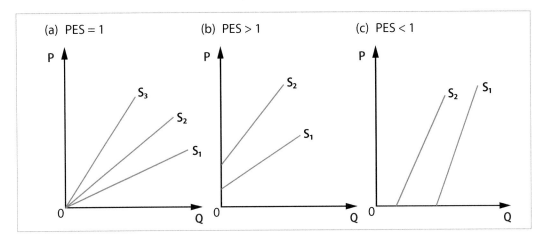

Figure 4.3: **Supply functions with varying price elasticity of supply**

Any supply that cuts the price axis will have elastic supply, any supply that cuts the quantity axis will have inelastic supply and any supply that passes through the origin will have unit elasticity regardless of slope.

With supply it is possible to have zero price elasticity for example whatever the price there will only be one Mona Lisa (Giaconda) painting. Less extreme examples are the supply of fresh fish on a given day or the supply of a food product that takes time to produce and cannot be stored. For some products that are produced in large quantities by many countries the world supply can be perfectly elastic (see section on international trade).

4.3.1 Factors that influence PES

▶   Time: whereas demand can adjust quite quickly, supply changes will generally take time depending on the length of the production period and the ability to store the product. Some agricultural crops take years to grow and some manufactured goods such as oil tankers take a long time to produce. It will thus take a few years for an increase in the price of avocados to bring about an increase in their supply.

▶   Spare capacity: if firms have spare capacity it will be much easier to increase supply than if they are working at full capacity.

▶   Speed of technological change: this factor, related to **time**, impacts the ability and cost of storing the product.

4.4 Applications of elasticity

Elasticity is a very important concept in economics and is likely to be tested in all of the exam papers with respect to its measurement, its determinants and its importance. Even if the question does not specifically ask for it, your knowledge of elasticity will frequently be an asset when evaluating effects of any price changes. This will be seen in Chapter 5 which examines government intervention in the market.

Chapter 5: Government Intervention in the market

Governments intervene in the market for a variety of reasons and in a number of ways. Such interventions will inevitably interfere with the allocative mechanism of the free market and will lead to a different allocation of resources. Whether these interventions lead to a better allocation of resources or not are an important evaluation point and you are encouraged to use real-world examples in order to make an objective assessment of the effects of government intervention. This is especially important since intervention is one of the key concepts.

5.1 Price controls

5.1.1 Maximum (Ceiling) Prices

Market prices are sometimes considered to be unaffordable (too high) for low income households. In the case of important items such as basic food, or rental accommodation the government might decide to restrict the price by imposing a maximum allowable price below the market equilibrium price. The effect of this is shown in Figure 5.1.

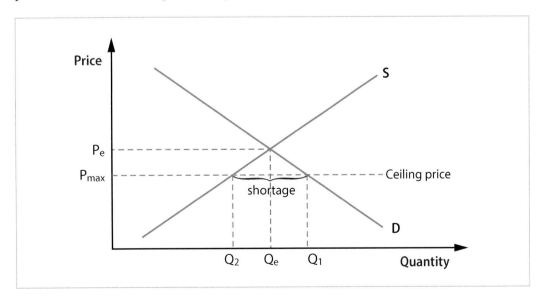

Figure 5.1: **Effect of a ceiling price**

As a result of the price ceiling the quantity demanded in the market will increase to Q_1 but quantity supplied will fall to Q_2. This leads to a shortage in the market equal to $Q_1 - Q_2$ such that some willing buyers will be unable to buy the good. As consumers compete with each other to secure the limited quantity available there will be pressure for a parallel market to develop in which the product will be illegally traded at higher prices. The price of the product in the parallel or unofficial market will be determined by the number of people willing to participate in the illegal trading and how easy it is for the market to operate.

In addition these markets will operate according to sellers preferences as the balance of power in the market will shift towards the sellers who have control over who to sell their products to. Real-world examples are the rent control policies that are widely applied in many US cities and in many areas of Germany. Tenants who are lucky enough to have controlled rents will benefit, but the negative effect on housing supply in the long run tends to increase housing costs for new tenants and the quality of housing will deteriorate as landlords are reluctant to pay for maintenance of rent controlled properties.

5.1.2 Minimum (Floor) Prices

A price floor, or minimum price, is an example of a price control imposed on the market for a good by the government. It makes it illegal to sell the good at a lower price than the specified minimum but will only affect the market if it is imposed above the existing market price.

There are various reasons why a government might choose to select this form of intervention:

- to ensure that the suppliers of a product are guaranteed a price which is sufficient to cover their costs and provide them with a satisfactory income. The implication here is that the market price would be too low to sustain production at a desired level;

- to introduce a greater degree of price stability in markets which are volatile such as certain agricultural markets;

- to increase the price of demerit goods in order to discourage consumption, as has been introduced for alcohol in Scotland in 2018 with the aim of preventing supermarkets from selling cheap alcoholic drinks.

The effect of minimum price controls is shown in Figure 5.2.

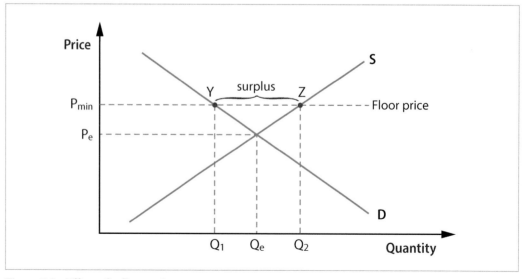

Figure 5.2: **Effect of a floor price**

A minimum price can act as a guaranteed price for farmers who otherwise would be faced with unstable incomes as market prices for many agricultural goods are subject to fluctuations. The effect is that the quantity supplied will increase to Q_2 while demand will fall to Q_1 and there will now be an excess supply in the market of $Q_2 - Q_1$. In order to maintain the price floor the government will have to remove the surplus from the market and this will involve the government buying it at the minimum price. The cost to the government will be equal to Q_1YZQ_2 and there may be further costs if the surplus is stored for future use.

Between 1960 and 1992 the EU as part of its Common Agricultural Policy (CAP) applied a guaranteed minimum price policy on a variety of agricultural goods which led to huge surpluses that eventually had to be disposed of.

A special case of minimum price controls is the case of a minimum wage which is applied in many countries. In this case the excess supply YZ represents an increase in unemployed workers as there are Q_2 willing to work at the minimum wage but only Q_1 jobs available.

It is interesting to note that despite the prediction based on economic theory that minimum wages lead to an increase in unemployment, there is evidence that in practice this is not always the case. In fact, according to a National Employment Law Project study for the USA in 2016, a review of seven decades of historical data found no correlation between minimum wage increases and employment levels.

5.2   Indirect Taxes

Indirect taxes are taxes on expenditure and are imposed either as a specific amount per unit such as the taxes on cigarettes in the UK or as a percentage of price such as VAT that is applied in many countries and are known as *ad valorem* taxes.

The imposition of a tax has the effect of increasing the costs of production for suppliers and this will cause a shift of supply to the left by the amount of the tax. In the case of a specific tax the shift will be parallel but for an *ad valorem* tax it will diverge as price rises.

There are two main reasons for the imposition of indirect taxes; the first is the general aim of taxation which is to gain revenue for the government. The second is to influence the consumption of a good. This will be considered in more detail in the section on market failure.

Exam questions will frequently link the imposition of indirect taxes to elasticity of demand and supply, with an emphasis on PED. This involves a potentially confusing use of the slope of demand as an indication of PED in order to show the effect on price and quantity demanded following the imposition of a tax and also to illustrate the **incidence** of a tax on consumers and producers. This refers to the way in which the burden of the tax is shared between consumers and producers.

The relevant diagrams that you are expected to present are shown in Figure 5.3.

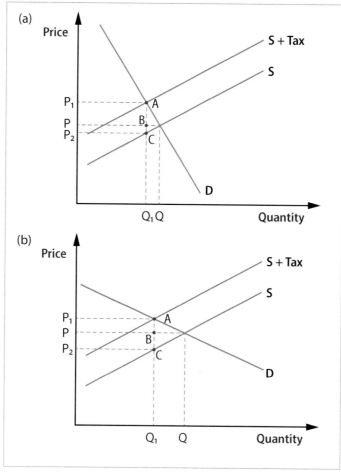

Figure 5.3: **Incidence of an indirect tax**

For IB exams you are expected to draw a steep demand function to illustrate inelastic demand and a flatter one to illustrate elastic demand. Figure 5.3(a) shows that the imposition of a tax on a product with an inelastic demand will have a greater incidence on consumers than producers (AB > BC) while (b) shows the opposite with an elastic demand (AB < BC). The total tax revenue to the government is equal to $P_2 P_1 AC$ in both diagrams.

PES will also influence the incidence of an indirect tax. The more elastic the supply the greater the incidence on consumers and the more inelastic the supply the greater the incidence on producers. With a perfectly inelastic supply the producer will pay all the tax and with a perfectly elastic supply the consumer will pay all the tax.

An astute student will notice an apparent inconsistency with regard to elasticity and the slope of the demand function. As seen in Figure 4.1 on page 11, elasticity varies along any downward sloping linear demand irrespective of the actual slope with unit elasticity at the mid-point, inelastic below it and elastic above it.

Both demand functions in Figure 5.3 will therefore have this range of elasticity so it is technically incorrect to describe them as inelastic and elastic.

The IB sidesteps this problem by referring to Figure 5.3 (a) as relatively inelastic (since the section of demand happens to be below the mid-point) and Figure 5.3 (b) as relatively elastic (since the section of demand happens to be above the mid-point).

Unfortunately the IB examiners have not yet responded to my question regarding how they would mark an answer that claimed that elasticity of demand has no influence on the incidence of a tax if Figure 5.4 was used to illustrate this, and in fact it is more relevant to consider the elasticity of supply in relation to demand.

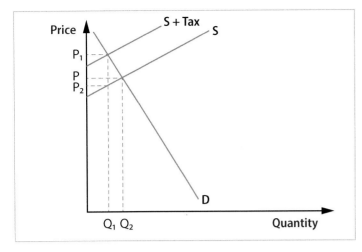

The demand in Figure 5.4 has the same slope as the demand in Figure 5.3 (a) but the tax is now imposed on the elastic section of demand. The incidence of the tax, however, is exactly the same as in Figure 5.3 which has the tax imposed on the inelastic section of demand.

Figure 5.4: **Incidence of an indirect tax on the elastic section of demand**

5.3 Subsidies

These are payments made by the government, usually to producers, which reduce their costs of production leading to a decrease in price and an increase in quantity as shown in Figure 5.5.

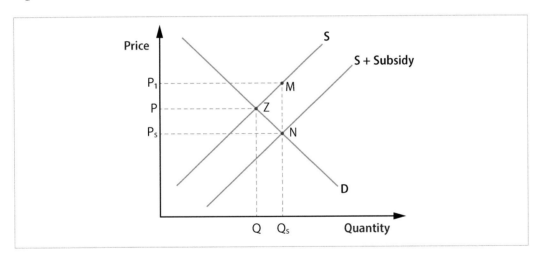

Figure 5.5: **The effect of granting a subsidy**

The subsidy will cause the supply to shift to the right leading to a decrease in price to P_s and an increase in quantity to Q_s. The cost to the government is equal to P_sP_1MN and the revenue to producers will increase from $OPZQ$ to OP_1MQ_s. Consumers will now be buying more at a lower price and will gain additional consumer surplus (see next section). Whether consumers will end up spending more or less on the subsidised good depends on the relative elasticity of demand.

5.4 Evaluation of Government Intervention in the Market

In order to evaluate or discuss the effects of any government intervention in the market it is necessary to consider first of all what the purpose of the intervention is and to what extent it is justified. For example as will be seen in the next section there is a potential justification for intervention whenever there is evidence of **market failure**. However, justification for intervention does not mean that any form of intervention is suitable or appropriate. Whether they are or not will depend on the actual examples and real-world situations. It can be claimed that maximum price controls on basic food although well intentioned, will not actually solve the affordability problem faced by low income household without any measures that will guarantee access to the products e.g. with an effective system of rationing. Low income households will not be able to participate in the parallel market. It is possible that a government intervention might actually make the situation worse in which case it can be described as a government failure. Many economists consider rent controls to be such an example as they fail to solve the housing problem and actually make the shortage worse.

You are encouraged to examine alternative viewpoints in the exam and as long as you support a particular view with evidence and appropriate theory your views will be accepted and rewarded. If however, you are supporting the view that price controls do not work or that they make situations worse, you should try to come up with a better alternative. For example, if the aim of the intervention is to make food more affordable for low income households there might be better policies than price controls such as food subsidies or income supplements or food vouchers (stamps). Subsidising food is often seen as a better alternative to a maximum price but it represents a blanket policy rather than a targeted policy because it makes food more affordable for everyone including high income households. If the policy aims to help low income households it should target these, which is why a policy of income supplements or food stamps might be better although these policies are not without problems.

Taxes and subsidies also distort market signals and will have effects on the markets for substitutes and complements of the taxed or subsidised products.

Chapter 6:   Market Failure

This is an important topic and is likely to be examined in all of the exam papers. It refers to the ability of the free market mechanism to achieve an efficient allocation of resources. As noted in the section on the key concepts, efficiency is a broad concept in economics with many aspects. For this section market failure will be defined as the inability of the market to achieve an optimum allocation of resources that maximises the combined consumer and producer surplus which is described as the social or community surplus. These concepts are illustrated in Figure 6.1.

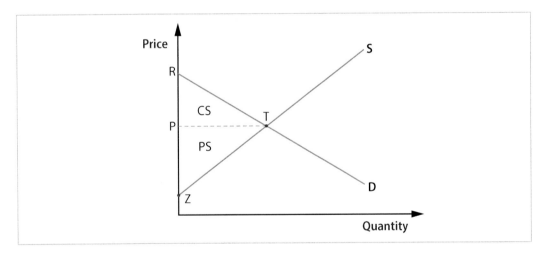

Figure 6.1: **Consumer surplus and producer surplus**

Consumer surplus (PRT) is the difference between what consumers are willing to pay and the amount that they actually pay and producer surplus (PTZ) is the difference between the price that producers are willing to sell their product and the price that they actually sell it for.

Types of market failure:

- Externalities
- Merit/Demerit goods
- Public Goods
- Asymmetric Information
- Monopoly power

In addition although technically not an example of market failure this section also considers the problem of **common access resources** and their link to the important key concept of sustainability.

6.1 Externalities

These are effects on third parties resulting from transactions between two parties or alternatively spillover effects on society generated by market transactions. The source of the externality can be either the **production** or **consumption** side of the market and it can either be positive (**external benefit**) or negative (**external cost**).

6.1.1 Negative production externality

This refers to situations where the production of a good imposes costs on society. An example is when the generation of electricity is achieved by burning fossil fuels such as coal or oil which lead to carbon emissions and atmospheric pollution. Carbon and other gas emissions are increasingly recognised to be a mounting health risk and contribute to the global problem of climate change and warming. If the social costs are not faced by the producer there will be a market failure of over production as shown in Figure 6.2.

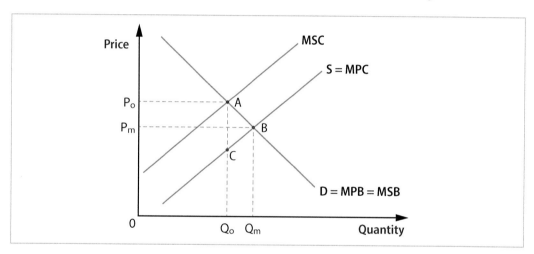

Figure 6.2: **Negative externality of production**

In a free market, price will be set at Pm where demand represented by the marginal private benefit (MPB) = supply represented by the marginal private cost (MPC) and the corresponding output will be at Q_m. This market equilibrium however, fails to take account of the cost that is imposed on society which is represented by the marginal social cost (MSC). This leads to a market failure of overproduction equal to Q_oQ_m and a welfare loss represented by the triangle ABC. The optimum allocation of resources is with production at Q_o and a price of P_o.

Positive production externalities are not usually asked for in the exam but if you need to discuss an example you can refer to the production of honey because the bees help to pollinate the farmer's crops which provides them with a benefit. Diagrammatically, you just need to switch MPC with MSC and $P_m Q_m$ with $P_o Q_o$.

6.1.2 Negative consumption externality

This occurs when the consumption of a good by one person imposes costs on another person or on society in general. Examples include the consumption of cigarettes, alcohol, petrol cars, unhealthy food and sugary drinks some of which are also classified as demerit goods. With consumption externalities the cost to society is shown by the divergence between the marginal private benefit to the consumer and the lower marginal social benefit to the rest of society. The demerit good of tobacco consumption for example, imposes various costs on society as a result of passive smoking and also the health problems faced by smokers are not confined to them but are faced by the whole society through higher health care costs and loss of productivity through ill health of the smokers. These costs are shown in Figure 6.3.

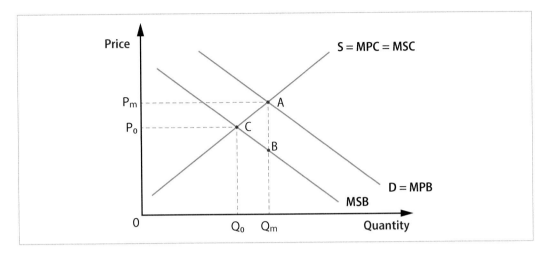

Figure 6.3: **Negative externality of consumption**

The free market will equate demand (MPB) with supply (MPC = MSC) and there will be a total of Q_m consumed which represents a market failure of overconsumption as the optimum quantity is Q_0. There will now be a welfare loss represented by the area ABC.

6.1.3 Positive consumption externality

This occurs when the consumption of a product confers benefits to the rest of society. Examples include health care and education which are also designated as merit goods. With the current pandemic it is evident that when an individual receives a vaccination not only does that person benefit but everyone benefits by the reduction of transmission risk and the development of herd immunity. Similarly, the consumption of education brings wider benefits to the whole society through increased productivity and higher living standards. The welfare gains from the consumption of such merit goods are shown in Figure 6.4.

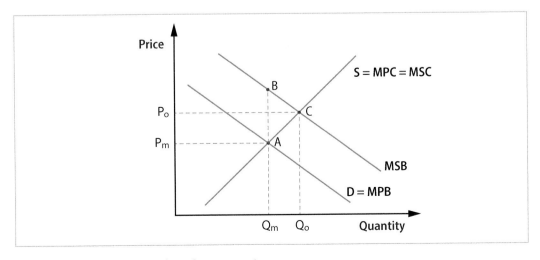

Figure 6.4: **Positive externality of consumption**

In a free market there will be under consumption below the social optimum represented by Q_mQ_o because equilibrium will be where demand (MPB) = supply (MPC + MSC). As a result there will be a welfare loss represented by the area ABC.

6.2 Government policies to reduce market failure resulting from externalities

There are two approaches that the government can take to address this problem:

▶ **Market based**

▶ **Rules and regulations**

Market based solutions aim to internalise the externality with policies that include the external cost or benefit with the private costs and benefits. For example, in the case of a negative consumption or production externality the cost to society could be added to the private costs with the imposition of an indirect tax the effect of which is as shown in figure 12.

An increasingly popular market based solution is the use of tradable permits or cap and trade schemes which aim to provide incentives for firms to reduce pollution levels and increase clean air efficiency. The permits allow only a restricted amount of pollution and if a firm is able to pollute less than the permit it can sell the difference to another firm. This encourages firms to develop and install less polluting technologies, while at the same time allowing the higher polluting firms to buy permits and remain in production, giving them more time to introduce cleaner technologies.

Subsidies can also be used as a market based solution to encourage the production and consumption of goods which have positive externalities. Norway for example provides generous subsidies towards the purchase of electric cars and in 2021 it was the leading country for electric car use with 54% of all cars.

Rules and regulations aim to encourage or discourage externality creating activities in a variety of ways. Many countries have introduced restrictions on smoking in public places and on the sale of tobacco and alcohol to people below a certain age. Barcelona has recently banned motorised vehicles from certain parts of the city and in most countries the consumption and sale of narcotics is illegal. Such regulations can be effective but they depend on how well they can be enforced. Sometimes it is possible to nudge consumers and producers to adapt their behavior by pre announcing the intention of a future policy change. For example, by announcing that it intends to ban the sale of petrol and diesel cars in 2035, the UK government is nudging consumers towards the purchase of electric cars.

In addition, market behavior can be influenced in the long-run through education as well as with negative advertising and awareness campaigns. Activists such as Greta Thunberg for example, have increased the level of awareness regarding the dangers of global warming and climate change.

Note that merit and demerit goods are special cases of externality and can be illustrated with the same diagrams as used for positive and negative consumption externalities.

6.3   Public goods

Unlike private goods, these goods are non-rivalrous and non-excludable. Once they are produced it is impossible to prevent anyone from consuming the product and one person's consumption in no way restricts anyone else's. Typical examples are lighthouses and national defence or an easily visible monument such as the Eiffel Tower. This non-excludability characteristic is what gives rise to the 'free rider' problem that makes it difficult if not impossible for a private company to provide public goods. For this reason it is normally the case that public goods are provided by the government and it is often thought that there is no efficient or effective alternative.

There are however, some cases where public goods can be provided through the market. Open TV and radio broadcasts are public goods that can be, and are, provided by the private sector with the cost being covered by advertising revenues. It is not inconceivable that a marine insurance company might decide to build a lighthouse in order to reduce the risk of accident claims. Despite the free rider problem it is also possible that community spirit might prevail and everyone will contribute to providing local public goods such as street lighting or neighbourhood watch. Finally, public goods such as monuments are sometimes provided by benefactors or individuals. An example is a mural created by a popular street artist such as Banksy.

Note that when the government decides to provide a public good it simply means that the cost will be covered by the government. The actual provision could be by a private company that is contracted by the government to provide it.

There are several misconceptions about the nature and provision of public goods.

Students often confuse 'public' anything, or anything provided free of charge by the state with public goods. Public (state) schools and public health are *not* examples of public goods. They are both rivalrous and excludable.

Similarly, roads and motorways are not pure public goods because they can become rivalrous when congested and are excludable. The fact that exclusion is not enforced does not make them public goods-the important principle is whether exclusion can be practiced.

Rather than claiming that roads or parks or museums are public goods it is more appropriate to describe them as **partial** or **quasi** public goods. In all these cases it is possible to exclude consumers and therefore to charge for access.

6.4   Asymmetric Information

This occurs when one side of the market has more information than the other side and can use this additional information to their advantage in a transaction. It is usually the supply side of the market that possesses the extra information. For example, a car mechanic can claim that a customer's car needs various things fixed for the safety of the vehicle and can take advantage of the customer's lack of mechanical knowledge to convince the customer to 'fix' them. Similarly, a dentist can invent procedures that need to be done to ensure oral health, taking advantage of most people's lack of dental knowledge.

An example of asymmetric information on the buyers side of the market is the case of a customer failing to disclose a potential genetic health problem when purchasing life insurance.

Potentially more serious cases are when industries create 'fake news' about their product or suppress information about the dangers of their product. Both the tobacco and the oil industry have been accused of such practices.

6.5 Common access or pool resources

These are natural resources which are non-excludable but rivalrous and will therefore tend to be over consumed, often to a level that is unsustainable. This over consumption is referred to as the 'tragedy of the commons' because common pasture land in rural areas was over grazed by cows and sheep. A similar situation has developed with over fishing in many of the world's oceans and seas which is recognised as being unsustainable. Other examples include deforestation, depletion of the ozone layer and destruction of the quality of air in the atmosphere.

Many of these sustainability issues are similar to problems created by negative production and consumption externalities and there is therefore a tendency to see the problem of overconsumption of common pool resources as an example of market failure. Technically, this is not correct however, because there is no market to begin with. It is a problem of missing markets rather than one of failing markets. The absence of a market is the result of the lack of property rights over common access resources. If an area of the sea was actually owned by someone it could be leased for fishing in the same way that an area of land can be leased for farming. Establishing property rights over common access resources is quite difficult and therefore remains a theoretical rather than a practical solution to the problem.

Since the most urgent issues of sustainability relating to over-consumption of common access resources are global, any effective solution relies on cooperation and agreement between countries. Such agreements, the most recent of which was the Paris Agreement signed by 196 countries in 2016, are very difficult to maintain especially when major polluters do not commit (for example, political divisions in the USA meant the country initially joined the Paris Agreement under President Obama, withdrew under President Trump, then re-admitted in 2021 following election of President Biden).

Many commentators consider such agreements to be ineffective as countries often claim to set targets but fail to meet them, and apart from attempts at public shaming there is little that the international community can do to ensure compliance. Newly industrialised countries like China and India also consider it to be unfair that they should be paying for past destruction to the environment caused by the developed countries.

Further complications are created by the climate change deniers and believers in 'fake news' which some environmental activists claim are promoted by business interests such as the fossil fuel industry.

Optimists put their faith in technology that they say will enable us to prevent a disastrous amount of global warming. While technological solutions such as methods of directly extracting carbon dioxide from the air will be part of the solution, many are only conceptual or experimental so the question remains whether these can be developed and reach scale in time.

6.6   **Monopoly power**

For the new syllabus, what used to be examined under the topic heading of the theory of the firm is now included as a market failure resulting from any lack of perfect competition in a market, and some aspects of firm's behaviour are examined under the 'behavioural economics' section of the new syllabus.

In the absence of any past papers there is no indication of the type of question that might be asked on this topic and the sample papers published by the IB had a conspicuous lack of any questions on any of the 3 papers relating to this topic. Whether future exams will actually have any theory of the firm questions remains to be seen. It is quite possible that the examiners will avoid the topic as it is unpopular with many teachers who find it difficult to teach and there was an attempt to remove the topic completely from the new syllabus but this was resisted by some curriculum advisors.

Monopoly power will be covered in this guide as an integrated theory of the firm rather than as a special case of market failure.

Chapter 7: Profit maximisation under different market structures

The traditional theory of the firm was developed on the assumption that the aim of a firm was to maximise its profit. When the typical firm was relatively small and the owner or risk taker was also the decision maker, this was a reasonable assumption to make. For a modern large company however, this assumption is considered to be an oversimplification of reality and modern behavioural theories of the firm have been developed which examine a variety of possible objectives that a firm might have other than profit maximisation.

These alternative objectives will be considered briefly later and for now market structures will be examined under the assumption of profit maximisation.

7.1 Profit

This is the difference between the total revenue (TR) from the sale of a firm's output and the total cost (TC) of producing that output. Economists identify two levels of profit:

▶ **Normal profit**: when TR = TC

▶ **Supernormal (Abnormal or Economic) profit**: when TR > TC

Normal profit is the amount that is necessary to keep the firm in operation and includes the reward or opportunity cost of the owner (entrepreneur) of the firm. It represents the break-even level.

Anything above this is more than necessary to keep the firm in business and would provide an incentive for new firms to enter the industry.

If TR < TC the firm will be making a loss.

7.2 Costs of production

As a firm increases its output TC will normally increase, but not all costs will change by the same amount or at the same rate.

Some costs are **fixed** and do not change with output in the **short run** while some costs are **variable** and change directly with output in the short run.

▶ **Fixed costs (FC)**: the costs of setting up the business and include the cost of the building and capital (machinery) and equipment.

▶ **Variable costs (VC):** the costs of operating the business and include the cost of raw materials, energy and direct labour.

The **short run** is the period when at least one factor of production is fixed so that it is only possible to change the **rate of production** while the **long run** is the period when all of the factors of production can be changed and therefore it is possible to change the **scale of production**.

Cost concepts: Total (T), Average (A) and Marginal (M)

$$TC = TFC + TVC$$

$$AFC = \frac{TFC}{Q}$$

$$AVC = \frac{TVC}{Q}$$

$$ATC = AFC + AVC$$

$$MC = \frac{\text{change in TC}}{\text{change in output by 1 unit}}$$

In the short run costs will change depending on the relative productivity of different combinations of fixed and variable factors. As more variable factors (such as workers) are combined with the fixed factors marginal product will initially increase as the principle of division of labour applies, but after a certain point it will necessarily be true that adding additional units of labour will eventually lead to decreasing marginal product as predicted by the **law of diminishing marginal returns**. The relationship between average and marginal product that is typically observed in the short run is shown in Figure 7.1.

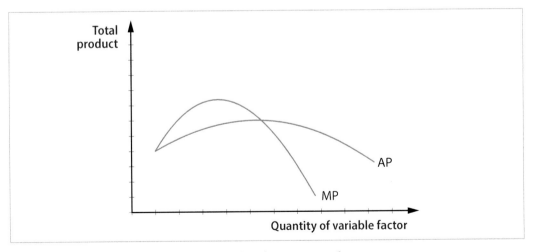

Figure 7.1: **Relationship between marginal and average product**

Note that MP will always cut AP from above at the highest point of AP. The point at which diminishing marginal returns set in is where MP begins to fall.

The variable costs of production in the short run will be the inverse of the product curves, as shown in Figure 7.2.

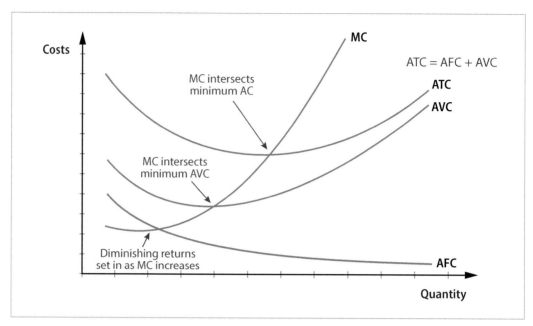

Figure 7.2: **Relationships between costs of production**

Figure 7.2 shows the relationships between the various cost concepts that apply in the short run. MC intersects with ATC at the minimum point of ATC and if a firm is operating at this point it will be breaking even and making normal profit. At any price above this point it will be making economic profit and at any price below this it will be facing a loss.

If a firm is facing a loss it needs to decide whether to shut down immediately or in the long run. The principle that is applied is that if it is able to cover its VC it should remain in production in the short run but if it is not able to cover VC it should shut down immediately. The point where MC intersects with AVC is therefore the shutdown point.

In the long run the firm is able to change the scale of production as it can change the fixed factors and therefore the costs in the long run will be determined by the efficiency of different scales of production (returns to scale).

It is normally the case that increases in scale will initially lead to a fall in ATC as a result of a variety of Economies of Scale (EOS), especially in large manufacturing industries such as car production. Eventually increasing returns will even out and further increases in scale may actually lead to increasing ATC as a result of Diseconomies of Scale (DOS). The typical sequence is shown in Figure 7.3.

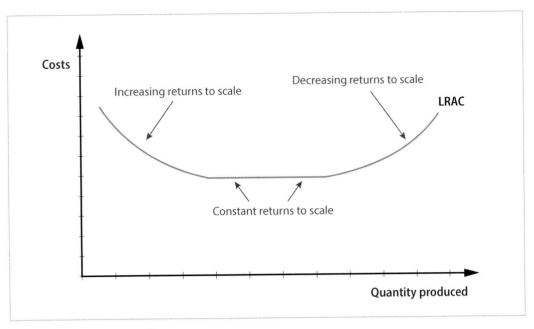

Figure 7.3: **Returns to scale**

Examples of EOS include:

- Technical economies through division of labour
- Bulk buying cost savings
- Economies of increased dimensions
- Financial economies

Examples of DOS include

- Loss of managerial efficiency
- Coordination problems
- Internal supply chain problems
- Increased exposure to ransomware attacks

In practice many large companies have considerable scope for earning cost advantages through exploiting EOS and will typically be operating with increasing or constant returns to scale.

7.3 Revenue from production

$$TR = P \times Q$$

$$AR = \frac{TR}{Q} = P$$

$$MR = \frac{\text{change in TR}}{\text{change in the sale of 1 unit}}$$

Note that AR is the price at which different quantities will be sold and therefore the AR is actually the demand function.

The relationship between TR, AR and MR is shown in Figure 7.4.

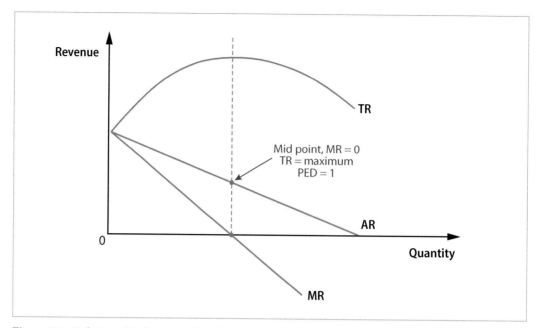

Figure 7.4: **Relationship between Total, Average and Marginal Revenue**

It is important to link the revenue concepts with elasticity and note that MR will always be zero at the mid-point of AR (Demand) where PED = 1 and TR is maximised. MR is positive where demand is elastic and negative where demand is inelastic.

7.4 Profit maximisation

A firm will always maximise its profit if it produces where MC = MR as shown in Figure 7.5.

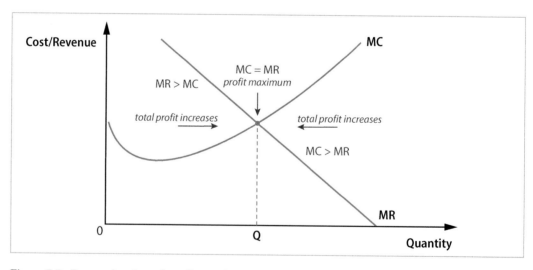

Figure 7.5: **Determination of profit maximisation**

The output where MC = MR will be where TR > TC by the greatest amount and will also be the loss minimising output for a loss-making firm.

7.5   Profit maximisation under different market structures

Perfect Competition

This was the original market structure that was examined by the classical economists and is considered to be a rather theoretical and idealised market with little practical relevance in the real-world. It exists under the following conditions:

- Large number of small firms
- Identical products
- Perfect freedom of entry into and exit out of the industry
- Perfect knowledge of the market

When all of the above apply the individual firm will be a price taker meaning that once the price has been set in the market every firm will be obliged to charge this price as they will face a perfectly elastic demand at the market price.

Short run equilibrium

A firm in perfect competition will be in short run equilibrium as long as it is producing its profit maximising output where MC = MR. This could be with economic profit, normal profit or a loss as long as it is covering its variable costs.

Long run equilibrium

As a result of the condition of perfect freedom of entry and exit neither economic profit nor losses can be maintained in the long run. In the case of economic profit there will be an incentive for new firms to enter the industry and as they enter the demand faced by each firm will fall until normal profit is established in the long run. This process is shown in Figure 7.6 (a) and (b).

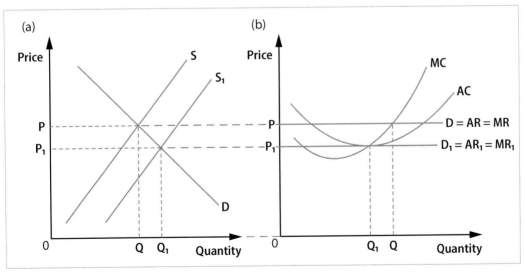

Figure 7.6: **Transition from short run to long run equilibrium in perfect competition**

In the case of short run losses the opposite process will occur with loss making firms leaving the industry so there is only one possible long run situation in perfect competition which is where every firm is earning only normal profit producing where MC = MR = AR = AC as shown in Figure 7.6 (b) at price P_1 and output Q_1. This long run equilibrium is important because it means that both allocative and productive efficiency are guaranteed since price = MC and output is at the lowest AC where MC = AC.

Monopoly

This is the opposite extreme to perfect competition and exists when there is one firm that is dominant in the industry producing a unique product in a market where there are effective barriers to entry. This means that the monopolist is able to set price and faces a downward sloping supply. A profit maximising monopolist will produce where MC = MR as shown in Figure 7.7.

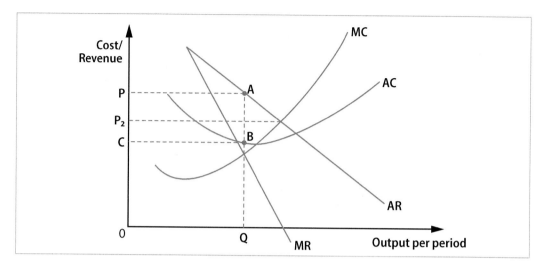

Figure 7.7: **Profit maximisation in monopoly**

The monopolist will produce output OQ where MC = MR and this output will be sold at price OP and the monopolist will be making economic profit equal to the area PABC. These economic profit levels will provide an incentive for competitors to enter but the existence of effective barriers to entry will prevent this so the monopolist will be able to maintain economic profit in the long run.

The monopolist will not be able to achieve allocative or productive efficiency because a downward sloping demand means that AR > MR so where MC = MR AR > MC. In Figure 7.6 if the industry was perfectly competitive and faced the same costs, the price would be at P_2 and allocative efficiency would be guaranteed. This is why monopoly is considered to be an example of market failure because price will always be above MC and there will be a welfare loss as a result. In the past most examples of monopoly were from the state sector, but since the 1980s many state monopolies have been privatised. Examples of pure monopolies with 100% of the market are rare in the private sector, but there are several examples of companies that are very dominant in their industry such as Dolby sound systems, Google and Luxottica (spectacles).

Monopolistic Competition

This market structure was developed during the 1930s in an attempt to introduce a more realistic element to the theory of the firm. It exists under the following conditions:

- Many small firms in the industry
- Each firm produces a similar but differentiated product
- There are no barriers to entry

This means that firms will be price makers like a monopoly as they face a downward sloping demand but since each firm has many close competitors prices will tend to be quite similar.

Short run equilibrium can exist with economic profit, normal profit or losses but in the long run the absence of barriers means that only normal profit can be maintained.

A short run equilibrium with economic profit will be as that of the monopoly shown in figure 25, but this will attract the entry of new firms and as they enter the demand faced by existing firms will shift to the left and the process will continue until there is no further incentive for new firms to enter when all firms are earning only normal profit as shown in Figure 7.8.

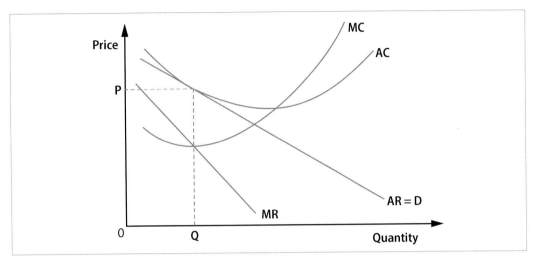

Figure 7.8: **Long-run equilibrium in monopolistic competition**

Loss making firms in either monopoly or monopolistic competition will close down in the long run. Figure 7.9 shows such loss making firms.

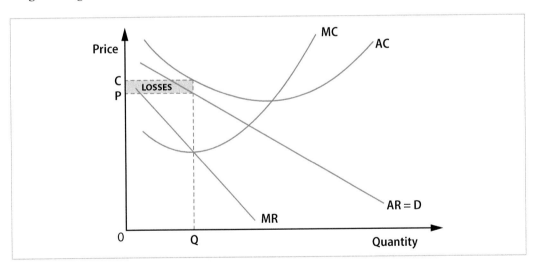

Figure 7.9: **Short run losses in monopolistic competition**

Examples of monopolistic competition are fast food restaurants, hairdressers, clothes shops and grocers. Although these types of firm are quite numerous, with respect to their value of output and contribution to the economy they are not very significant. Even though they provide a more realistic and numerous example of actual real-world businesses than perfect competition, examples of which are almost exclusively confined to some agricultural markets, monopolistic competition is still not that relevant in developed economies. The dominant market structure in terms of value of output and contribution to the economy in such economies is by far oligopoly.

Oligopoly

This is by far the most important and realistic market structure in developed economies and exists when the market is dominated by a few large firms. This market domination is measured by concentration ratios which examine the share of a market between a given number of firms. For example a 3-firm concentration ratio of 80% means that the 3 largest firms in the industry between them control 80% of the market. The remaining 20% might be shared between 100 firms, but the large number of firms does not make the market an example of monopolistic competition. The same applies to markets that have many different brands such as beer and household detergents. In these cases there are a few firms that between them produce a wide variety of brands; the global market for detergents and household cleaning products is dominated by two companies, Unilever and Procter & Gamble.

Oligopolists normally produce differentiated products and operate in markets which have high barriers to entry, frequently created by the firms themselves, such as brand proliferation that saturates the market with choice.

Oligopoly is unique because each firm is large enough to influence the market on its own but not large enough to be able to ignore the actions of rival firms. This creates a high degree of interdependence between the firms and this determines many of the characteristics of oligopolistic markets.

Collusion

Interdependence means that if one firm changes its price it cannot be certain of the result because this depends on the reactions of rival firms. This uncertainty leads to a general desire to avoid price competition because such competition could lead to a price war that would be damaging to all firms.

The best way of avoiding price competition is through agreements, but any formal agreements are illegal and are defined as a cartel. The practical alternative is for the collusion to be either secret or tacit which makes it difficult for the authorities to detect. Sometimes the need for any agreement is unnecessary if there is a dominant firm that acts as a price leader which the other oligopolists are willing to follow.

Non-collusive behaviour

The incentive for firms to collude is strongest when there are fewer firms in the industry and when the products are quite similar. In industries with more than 3 or 4 large firms and more especially if they produce highly differentiated products there is less of an incentive to collude. An example would be the car industry which typically has between 5 and 8 large firms and characteristically has rather large price differences for similar types of car. In contrast the UK Competition and Markets Authority in the UK fined 3 concrete companies 36 million pounds in 2019 for price fixing. Their products are virtually identical.

In Europe and the UK supermarkets have been accused and fined for price fixing as well as banks and real estate companies.

Even if there is no collusion between oligopolists, there is still an incentive to avoid price competition based on the high degree of interdependence. This avoidance can be explained by an application of game theory which shows that the default strategy of rivals is to maintain prices rather than risk a price war. An alternative explanation is provided by the kinked-demand curve theory which is attractive as a theory but has little practical accuracy since empirical studies have resoundingly shown that oligopolists pursue a cost plus pricing policy.

Actual pricing policies in oligopoly are in practice quite complex and as such are outside the scope of pre undergraduate level economics.

The kinked demand curve is a convenient method for explaining the characteristic of price rigidity in oligopoly based on the expected reaction of rivals to one firms pricing initiatives. The fact that it also shows price rigidity in the face of relatively large changes in costs is what makes it incorrect as a valid theory since it is observed that oligopolists do change price in response to cumulative cost changes which is consistent with the cost plus system of pricing where price is set as a percentage mark up on the average cost.

A collusive oligopoly effectively acts like a monopoly so the monopoly diagram (Figure 7.7 on page 34) can be used to illustrate profit maximisation, and like a monopoly the existence of barriers to entry means that any economic profit in the short run can be maintained in the long run.

Given the avoidance of price competition, it would be expected that oligopolists would try to increase market share through various forms of non-price competition such as advertising, special offers, free gifts, etc.

Comparison between market structures

Traditional comparisons tended to support perfect competition as an ideal market structure which was more desirable than monopoly because it guaranteed both allocative and productive efficiency and if faced with the same costs a perfectly competitive industry would always have a lower price and a higher output than a monopoly. In Figure 7.7 the monopoly price is P while the competitive price is P_2.

A more modern and realistic treatment of this topic however, casts considerable doubt on the traditional view and there are many important factors that need to be considered when comparing and evaluating market structures. The criteria that need to be considered are:

- Efficiency (Allocative and Productive)
- Price and output
- Variety, choice and quality
- Dynamic efficiency resulting from research & development (R&D) leading to innovation and dynamic economic growth

With respect to allocative and productive efficiency perfect competition will always be superior to all other market structures because no other will achieve them. It is the absence of allocative efficiency that leads to the market failure in any non-perfectly competitive market structure.

With respect to price and output perfect competition will only be superior to monopoly if costs of production are the same as in the comparison in figure 25. A realistic comparison however, is that if a perfectly competitive industry became a monopoly there would be a significant reduction in costs as a result of rationalisation of production and considerable EOS. This could therefore lead to lower prices and a higher output. The same would also apply with the industry becoming an oligopoly.

With respect to variety and choice these will never exist in perfect competition and will only be a feature of markets with differentiated products such as the two examples of imperfect competition-monopolistic and oligopoly.

For dynamic efficiency there needs to be both an incentive and ability for firms to engage in R&D. The fact that only markets that can earn economic profit in the long as a result of entry barriers will have such ability and incentives makes dynamic growth more likely with large dominant firms than with small competitive firms with only long run normal profit.

Whether a particular market structure is preferable or not will depend on the emphasis that is given to the criteria identified above. Are consumers more interested in allocative efficiency or with choice, quality and price? Would a perfectly competitive industry such as oranges or soya beans generate more dynamic growth through R&D and innovations than oligopolies such as car production, computers and smart phones?

If search engines were perfectly competitive with hundreds of small firms would they provide a cheaper and better service than Google's monopoly? Would converting a natural monopoly, like railways or water supply to houses, to a perfectly competitive industry bring about any benefits? Do high street grocers provide a cheaper product and more efficient service than oligopolistic supermarkets? These are the type of questions that need to be considered and the answers may vary from country to country and depend on the examples used and people's personal opinions.

The theory of the firm is one of the most interesting and relevant aspects of economics and has major implications for how the macro economy operates and what macro- economic model is more realistic (though this is not covered in the IB syllabus).

To answer questions on the exam effectively requires the ability to illustrate with appropriate fully explained diagrams together with relevant real-world examples. Although for the IB it might appear that the most important feature of the topic is the market failure of monopoly due to lack of allocative efficiency, you should try to take a broader approach as outlined in the comparison above.

The IB welcomes alternative viewpoints as long as they are backed up with appropriate evidence and valid theories which correspond to relevant examples.

Whether the examiners will acknowledge that allocative efficiency is an all or nothing concept and that it is therefore not possible to have more of it or less of it remains an unknown and for safety it might be wise to follow the syllabus and consider monopolistic competition to be less inefficient than monopoly even though it fails to achieve allocative efficiency and will always be productively inefficient in long run equilibrium without any scope for lower costs through EOS.

7.6 Behavioural theories

These are alternative theories of a firm's objectives to those of profit maximisation. They have developed largely as a result of the separation of ownership from control that is typical of the modern large corporation. The owners are the shareholders and the decision makers are the executives and managers. This separation means that the decision makers will not necessarily pursue profit maximisation but will be motivated by other considerations such as revenue maximisation or sales maximisation depending on what bonus incentives they might have. Another possibility is that decisions might be based on achieving a satisfactory level of profit rather than chasing maximum profit. This is known as satisficing and is considered to be a widespread practice in real life.

In addition, there are firms or companies that operate as non-profit organisations whose aim is simply to provide some social or humanitarian service. An increasing number of firms are becoming concerned with their image and will sometimes be willing to sacrifice profit for a better association with social responsibility e.g. Bombas sock producer donates a pair to someone in need for every pair that is sold, the same policy is followed by Warby Parker which makes eye glasses. A vast number of companies also support local community projects and donate to charities and non-profit organisations. For many firms such socially responsible behavior may be altruistic but brand image is also very important for future profitability.

Government intervention to promote competition

Given the market failure associated with the abuse of monopoly power the government has a policy aimed at restricting or reducing this potential anti-competitive behavior. This mainly involves rules and regulations that seek to prevent price fixing and collusion. In addition, privatised monopolies in the UK are subject to restrictions on their pricing policies.

Potential monopolies are defined by law, in the UK as any firm with at least 25% of the market, and can be investigated if suspected of operating against the consumer's interests. The anti-monopoly laws will also allow investigation of proposed mergers between firms in case they will restrict competition at the expense of consumers. This type of legislation is quite complex and difficult to enforce and evaluate, and despite persistent claims that social media platforms such as Google and Facebook abuse their monopoly positions no action has been taken against them in either the USA or Europe.

It should be noted however, that in the case of 'natural monopolies' that are able to exploit all available EOS and operate at a minimum LRAC increasing or encouraging competition would not be advantageous as the cost advantage would be lost.

Chapter 8: Equity and Equality

Equity and equality refer to the distribution of income in the economy, which will always be unequal in a free market economy, and if this level of inequality is relatively large it might also be considered to be inequitable. This is a subjective value judgment implying that it is unfair. A high degree of income inequality is considered by some economists and governments to be a market failure that needs some form of correction. The appropriate policies for making income distribution more equal and more equitable will be examined in the section on macroeconomics.

Chapter 9:   Macroeconomics

This is concerned with the economy as a whole and how the level of economic activity is measured and determined together with the government's policy objectives and ways in which it aims to achieve these objectives. Whereas microeconomics is concerned with the establishment of equilibrium in individual markets, macroeconomics is concerned with the establishment of equilibrium in the entire economy.

9.1   The measurement of economic activity

Economic activity can only be effectively measured as a value and this is expressed as **National Income** which represents the total value of all goods and services produced in an economy over a specified period of time such as a year or a quarter. There are 3 alternative ways of measuring this each of which should provide the same value:

National Income = National Output = National Expenditure

Any of these methods will provide a measure referred to as **Gross Domestic Product (GDP)** which is the total value of all goods and services produced with domestic factors of production in a given period. **Gross National Income (GNI)** is a wider measure that includes net property income from abroad.

GNI = GDP + inflows of property income – outflows of property income.

These values can be expressed as nominal or money amounts or as is more useful as real values which represent nominal values adjusted for inflation. The following formula should be used for numerical calculations:

$$\text{Real Income} = \frac{\text{Nominal Income}}{\text{Deflator}} \times 100$$

There is also a concept of **Green GDP** which adjusts the GDP for environmental degradation and is increasingly becoming an important measure given the current threat of climate change and global warming.

In all economies the accurate measurement of national income is difficult and there are a variety of problems that are typically encountered such as the value of unpaid services and the size of the informal or unrecorded economy. When comparing statistics for different countries and relating these to living standards and quality of life further complications arise such as the distribution of income, the purchasing power of income, the composition of output as well as a wide range of social and political factors.

9.2　The concept of the circular flow

Income is not a static amount but is a flow which is generated through transactions between households (H) and firms (F) as shown in Figure 9.1.

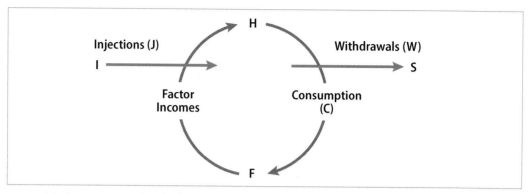

Figure 9.1:　**Income as a circular flow**

Households receive factor incomes from their contribution to production in the form of wages to labour, rent to land, interest to capital and profit to the entrepreneur. This income when spent on the produce of firms will be received as income which will be used for further consumption spending and so on. Realistically some income received will not be spent but will be saved and this will release some resources from consumer goods production to be used for the production of capital goods. This spending by firms on capital is described as investment and represents an additional spending or injection (J) into the circular flow and in a closed economy with no government it will be equal to the amount of savings (S) that is a withdrawal (W) from the circular flow.

In this simplified model equilibrium will be established when J = W, which in this case means I = S. In a more realistic model with a government sector and which is open to international trade there will be additional injections in the form of government spending (G) and exports (X) with corresponding withdrawals of taxation (T) and imports (M). Now, equilibrium will be established when planned J = planned W or alternatively when:

$$I + G + X = S + T + M$$

If J > W the level of income will rise until a new higher equilibrium is reached and vice versa if W > J.

 Note that the equilibrium condition does not require each pair of J and W to be equal, just the totals.

9.3　How to analyse macroeconomic equilibrium

Macroeconomic analysis is conducted with the use of different models that apply the concepts of **aggregate demand (AD)** and **aggregate supply (AS)**.

AD represents the total demand in the economy and is made up of:

- consumption (C)
- investment (I)
- government spending (G), and
- exports (X) – imports (M)

$$AD = C + I + G + (X - M)$$

There are no differences between the various schools of economic thought regarding the nature of AD, as all recognise it to be downward sloping as shown in Figure 9.2.

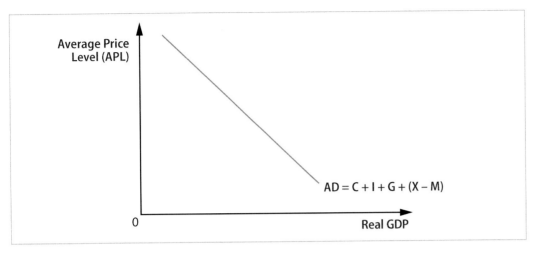

Figure 9.2: **The components of aggregate demand (AD)**

The components of AD

Consumption: the total spending by households on goods and services which will be influenced by:

- disposable income (positively related)
- interest rates (negatively related)
- wealth (positively related)
- consumer confidence (positively related)

Investment: the total spending by firms on capital such as machinery and buildings, which will be influenced by:

- business confidence (positively related)
- interest rates (negatively related)

Government spending: the total spending by the government on health care, education, defense, salaries of public employees, welfare and infrastructure, which will be influenced by:

- political commitments
- policy requirements

Exports: the total value of all transactions that give rise to inflows of currency, which will be influenced by:

- incomes in other countries
- the relative prices of traded goods determined by domestic prices and the exchange rate of the currency

Imports: the total spending by domestic households that gives rise to outflows of currency, which will be determined by:

- domestic income
- the relative prices of traded goods determined by domestic prices and the exchange rate of the currency

Any increase in any component of AD will cause it to shift to the right and vice versa.

With AS, which represents the total value of all domestic production, it is necessary to distinguish between the short run AS (SRAS) and the long run AS (LRAS). The SRAS is upward sloping with respect to the average price level as it reflects the collective behavior of all firms in the economy while the LRAS will be vertical at the full employment level of income as this represents the maximum potential output of the economy. It corresponds to the PPC concept in the introduction to microeconomics.

The two main models applied in macroeconomics are:

- **Keynesian**; and

- **neoclassical/monetarist**.

They differ with respect to their underlying assumptions regarding the microeconomic models of market behaviour that they use. This determines how, and how quickly, the economy responds to demand shocks, but first it is necessary to examine what can cause shifts in SRAS and LRAS.

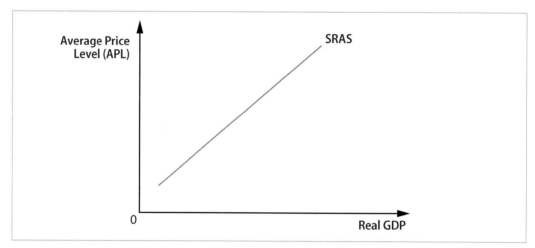

Figure 9.3: **Short run aggregate supply**

The SRAS will shift to the left in response to any change in the costs of production which could be the result of:

- A general increase in wages

- An increase in the prices of oil and raw materials

- An increase in indirect taxes on expenditure

The opposite of any of these will cause SRAS to shift to the left

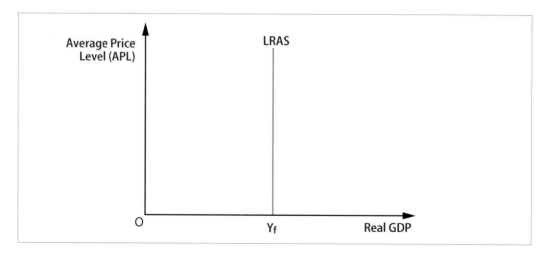

Figure 9.4: **Long run aggregate supply**

Y_f represents the full employment level of output which corresponds to the natural rate of unemployment (Y_n) and is the amount of unemployment that exists when the labour market is in equilibrium.

The LRAS will shift in response to any changes in either the quantity or the quality of the factors of production which is exactly what can cause the PPC to shift, for example any of the following will cause the LRAS to shift to the right:

- a discovery of mineral deposits (Land);
- an increase in immigration (Labour);
- an increase in investment by firms (Capital);
- training of workers (Labour);
- grants for setting up new businesses (Entrepreneur).

Keynesian vs Neoclassical AS

According to the Keynesian model the slope of the AS will depend on where the economy is operating. At low levels of real GDP the AS will be horizontal since firms will be operating with excess capacity and will be willing and able to increase output without needing to be induced to do so with higher prices. Since factors of production are widely available they can be hired at existing price levels. As the economy approaches Y_f the AS will be upward sloping as increases in output will require firms being able to attract factors of production which will put pressure on prices to rise. Finally, when the economy is operating at Y_f then AS will be vertical as this represents the long run situation when output cannot be increased. A typical Keynesian AS is shown in Figure 9.5.

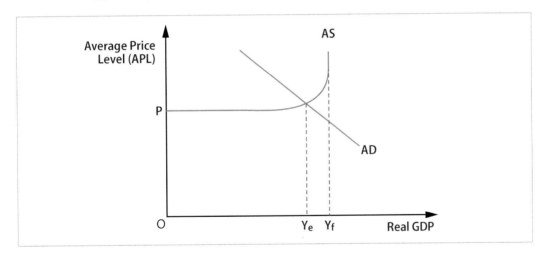

Figure 9.5: **A typical Keynesian aggregate supply curve**

According to the neoclassical model the economy will always operate in the long run at the full employment level of income Y_f, where LRAS is vertical and any divergence from this will only be temporary because the free market mechanism will work to automatically restore long run equilibrium at Y_f.

The significance of the differences between the two models is that in the Keynesian model equilibrium income (Y_e) will be established wherever AD = AS and that there is no automatic mechanism that will move the equilibrium to Y_f even if $Y_e < Y_f$. In contrast to this the neoclassical model predicts that if $Y_e < Y_f$ the economy will automatically adjust to restore equilibrium at Y_f.

If $Y_e < Y_f$ the situation is described as a deflationary or recessionary gap and is characterised by falling income, output and employment. In the Keynesian model such a situation will persist and there is therefore scope for the government to intervene in order to restore equilibrium at Y_f by shifting AD to the right. In the neoclassical model, however, such an intervention is unnecessary because the economy will automatically re-establish equilibrium at Y_f. The process by which this happens is shown in Figure 9.6.

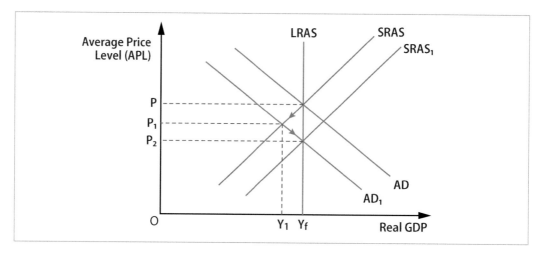

Figure 9.6: **Equilibrium readjustment in the neoclassical model**

Assuming that the economy is initially in long run equilibrium at Y_f with SRAS = AD = LRAS at price level P, a sudden decrease in AD to AD_1 will cause the equilibrium level of income to fall to Y_1 and the price level will fall to P_1. At these new levels there will be increased unemployment that will create downward pressure on wages and the lower price level will reduce costs of raw materials. As a result the costs of production faced by firms will fall and this will lead to a shift in SRAS to the right to $SRAS_1$. This will restore the long run equilibrium at Y_f and at a lower APL of P_2. In the Keynesian model this process will either not occur at all or will operate too slowly to be of any practical relevance so that government intervention is necessary to return the economy to Y_f.

For the exam you are only required to be able to illustrate these differences and explain them by stating that they are based on different scenarios relating to how the economy responds to demand shocks. You should be aware that the essential difference between the two models relates to whether prices and wages are fully flexible downwards. The neoclassical model believes that they are fully flexible in both directions while the Keynesian model believes that they are generally inflexible and especially downwards. You are not expected to be able to present an evaluation of which viewpoint is the most realistic as this would require the ability to link microeconomic theory of market structures to macroeconomic models. For wages and prices to be fully flexible it would require that markets are perfectly competitive and therefore adjust quickly to changes while for wages and prices to be inflexible or rigid it requires that markets are oligopolistic and characterised by price rigidity.

9.4 How to apply the AD/AS model

For all three papers you will be required to present some analysis relating to macroeconomic problems and solutions. This analysis will require an accurate use of diagrams showing causes and results of shifts in AD and/or AS. The important decisions will be:

- what shifts and in which direction;
- which model to use;
- how to evaluate the results of the shifts.

The context within which these decisions have to be made will be with respect to the *causes* of the problems, the *consequences* of the problem and the *cures* for the problems. For purposes of revision you need to concentrate on these '3 Cs' and how they are related to the government's policy objectives.

9.5 Objectives of government policy (Causes of problem)

The main macroeconomic objectives are:

- a low (2%) stable rate of inflation;
- an acceptable level of unemployment;
- a steady and sustainable rate of economic growth;
- an equitable distribution of income;
- a balance in the (X – M) component of AD (this topic will be covered in the section on international trade).

Inflation

This is defined as a persistent or continuous increase in the APL over time and can be caused by either increases in AD (demand-pull) or decreases in SRAS (cost-push) as shown in Figure 9.7.

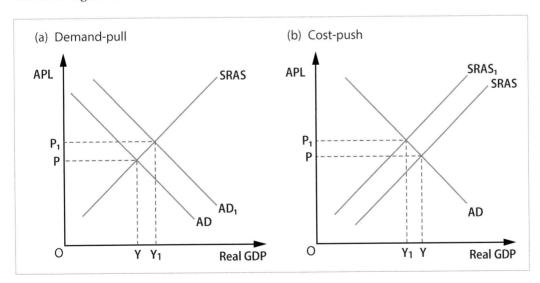

Figure 9.7: **Types of inflation**

If AD shifts to AD_1, as in Figure 9.7 (a), there will be an increase in the APL to P_1 which creates demand-pull inflationary pressure. At the same time there will be an increase in real GDP leading to an increase in income, output and employment.

If the economy faces any increase in the costs of production this will cause the SRAS to shift to $SRAS_1$ in Figure 9.7 (b) and as a result the APL will increase to P_1 and at the same time there will be a decrease in real GDP, output and employment to Y_1. This effect is referred to as 'stagflation' meaning an increase in inflation and unemployment at the same time.

Regardless of whether inflation is initiated by demand-pull or cost-push pressures, once an inflationary process is generated it is likely that the two will combine and if not controlled could stimulate expectations of inflation that will contribute a dynamic element to the inflationary process.

Unemployment

This is a measure of the percentage of the working population that is able and willing to work but is unable to find a suitable job. As with inflation, there are two types or causes of unemployment, equilibrium and disequilibrium, which relate to whether or not the labour market is in equilibrium.

▶ **Equilibrium unemployment**: includes all the unemployment that is part of the natural rate that is consistent with Y_f and the potential output of the economy. It is made up three separate types:

  – Frictional

  – Seasonal

  – Structural

Frictional refers to people who are in the process of changing jobs and is by definition confined to the short run and does not constitute a major problem. In developed economies which produce a wide variety of products, **seasonal** unemployment is not usually a big problem though for countries that depend heavily on seasonal tourism, like Greece, it can be a problem.

Structural unemployment is by far the most important example of equilibrium unemployment and is caused by any structural change in the demand for a particular skill or type of labour in the economy. Such changes can be the result of a technological innovation that replaces a manual job e.g. online holiday booking has reduced the demand for travel agencies and ticket sellers, robots have reduced the demand for car production line workers and music streaming has reduced the demand for CD producers and sellers.

It is important to separate the above causes of structural unemployment with the reasons that once created it persists. This is due to a mismatch between the unemployed workers and the available jobs in the economy. The mismatch is either geographical, meaning that the unemployed are in one place while the jobs are in another place, or occupational, meaning that the unemployed workers do not have the necessary skills to fill the available jobs.

The total amount of equilibrium unemployment should be roughly equal to the number of employment vacancies in the economy.

▶ **Disequilibrium unemployment**: exists when there are more unemployed workers than could fill all the available job vacancies meaning that there is insufficient demand in the economy to provide enough jobs. For example if there are 2 million unemployed and 1.5 million jobs available there will be half a million unemployed due to deficient demand. This demand deficiency is usually related to the recession phase of the trade cycle and is also referred to as **cyclical unemployment**. It is the type of unemployment associated with a deflationary or recessionary gap as shown in Figure 9.8.

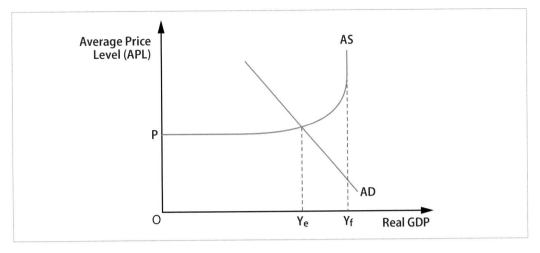

Figure 9.8: **Deflationary gap with cyclical unemployment**

The equilibrium level of income will be at Y_e where AD intersects with AS and this will be less than is necessary for full employment at Y_f. There is a deflationary gap $Y_e - Y_f$ which corresponds to cyclical unemployment.

Growth

This is a measure of changes in the level of economic activity over time as indicated by percentage changes in real GDP. There are two types of growth:

- **actual growth** is any increase in real income towards Y_f;
- **potential growth** is any increase in the full employment output.

Most countries will normally experience positive growth over time but the rate of growth will vary between countries and will fluctuate over time according to the trade or business cycle. The four phases of the cycle – **peak, recession, trough** and **recovery** – are shown in Figure 9.9.

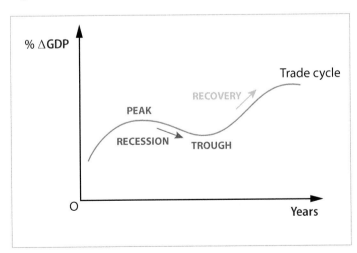

Figure 9.9: **Phases of the trade cycle**

The trade cycle is a recognised and regular feature of market economies and is on average completed every 8–10 years. In addition to these cyclical changes, the level of economic activity can also be affected by unexpected or sudden events. For example, two recent recessions were not related to the trade cycle but to external factors in the form of the financial crisis in 2008 (which caused a deep recession for two or more years in the global economy) and the recent Covid-19 pandemic from which the global economy is not expected to recover until 2022.

As an objective, governments generally want to achieve a high stable rate of growth, but increasingly this is linked to sustainability because high rates of growth are linked to increased emissions and environmental degradation.

Equity

This is more of a stated objective of governments rather than an actual objective since it is evident that since the 1980s the increase in income inequality, which may be seen as being unfair and therefore inequitable, has been the result of government policy measures aimed at promoting the free market and the supply side of the economy.

The exact extent of the problems caused by the lack of an equitable distribution of income is very difficult to quantify as they include economic, social and political factors. Some degree of income inequality is recognised as being unavoidable and even justified as it may simply reflect different contributions to the production process of different factors of production. However, extremes of inequality are increasingly drawing attention and in the most recent (June 2021) meeting of the G7 countries there is the likelihood of securing an agreement to a 15% tax on multinational companies in all of the countries where they operate, in the interests of equity.

The degree of income inequality in a country is illustrated by a Lorenz curve as shown in Figure 9.10.

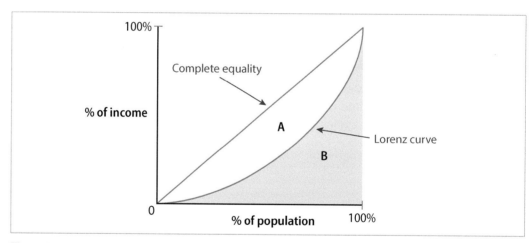

Figure 9.10: **Lorenz curve**

The closer that the Lorenz curve is to the line of complete equality, the more equal the distribution of income. This degree of inequality can also be expressed by reference to the Gini coefficient:

$$\text{Gini coefficient} = \frac{\text{Area A}}{\text{Area A} + \text{Area B}}$$

The higher the Gini coefficient, the more unequal the distribution of income.

9.6 Government policy to achieve the objectives (Cures)

In order to secure its policy objectives, the government has two policy approaches that it can apply:

▶ **Demand Side Policies (DSP)**

▶ **Supply Side Policies (SSP)**

DSP attempt to influence the level of economic activity by shifting AD while SSP attempts the same by shifting, AS and in particular LRAS.

Demand Side Policies

There are two ways in which AD can be influenced:

- Fiscal policy
- Monetary policy

Fiscal policy

This involves changes in government spending (G) relative to taxation (T). If the aim is to increase AD the policy will be expansionary and will require an increase in G relative to T and vice versa. These changes in $G/_T$ are also described as budget changes which refer to the government's spending and taxation plans for the financial year. An expansionary policy involves a budget deficit and a contractionary policy is one that will reduce the budget deficit or possibly create a budget surplus.

Monetary Policy

This policy is implemented by the Central Bank rather than the government, and involves the manipulation of the money supply in order to influence the rate of interest. Changes in the rate of interest will affect the cost of borrowing and the attractiveness of saving and will therefore influence any credit financed consumption and investment spending. Specifically, if interest rates are increased this will increase the cost of borrowing and increase the attractiveness of saving so both C and I will fall and as a result AD will shift to the left and vice versa. The process by which the central bank operates to influence interest rates in the money market is quite complex and there have been many modern developments such as quantitative easing (QE) which involves the central bank buying government debt in order to increase the liquidity of financial institutions such as the commercial banks that provide loans to individuals and businesses.

In some countries recently, in order to boost the economy which was becoming seriously depressed as a result of the pandemic, monetary policy has been used to directly finance government spending. This reflects a growing acceptance of modern monetary theory, as supported by economists such as Stephanie Kelton who argue that monetary policy can be used to finance government spending without fear of debt induced inflation. Mainstream economics/economists are reluctant to accept these developments and their implications and despite the notable absence of any inflationary pressures since the adoption of QE and other expansionary monetary measures since 2009, they still retain a pessimistic inflation phobia.

Supply side policies

There are two types of SSP approaches that are applied:

- Interventionist
- Market orientated

Interventionist policies are those which attempt to stimulate the supply side of the economy through government intervention in the form of spending support. For example:

- Training of workers
- Subsidies and grants for Investment and R&D
- Spending on infrastructure such as building roads, bridges and communications systems

Market orientated policies are those which aim to stimulate the supply side of the economy through reducing or removing the government from the economy and allowing a freer operation of the price mechanism. For example,

- Privatisation
- De-regulation of markets
- Restrictions on collusion
- Labour market reforms such as:
- Reduction or removal of minimum wages
- Reduction or removal of unemployment benefits and welfare payments
- Increased use of part-time working
- Reduction in power and influence of trade unions

These policies are expected to provide incentives for firms to increase production and compete more energetically and to give incentives to workers to find jobs more quickly and thus reducing the natural rate of unemployment. Additional SSP aiming to provide incentives for increased productivity and economic activity are tax changes that reduce progressive direct taxes in favour of indirect taxes. Even though such changes are recognised as leading to a less equal distribution of income they are favoured because they are claimed to promote greater efficiency by reducing the disincentive effect of progressive taxes.

A fuller evaluation of DSP and SSP will be completed later, for now the purpose is simply to identify the main policy alternatives available to governments in order to achieve their objectives.

Perceptive students might be asking the pertinent question: *What is the difference between interventionist SSP and Fiscal Policy that is a DSP?*

I personally disagree with the practice of baptising definitive examples of expansionary fiscal policy, such as road building, as SSP simply because they also have an effect on the supply side of the economy. It would be much more accurate to recognise these policies as DSP (fiscal policies) that as well as causing AD to increase will also cause LRAS to increase.

This is in fact a very good evaluation point to use when assessing the relative effectiveness of different macro policies to achieve government objectives. You are expected to be able to identify demand side effects of SSP and supply side effects of DSP.

9.7 Applying the cures to the causes

Here I want to provide a simple framework that can be applied to answering the very popular and typical Paper 1 part (b) questions regarding the relative effectiveness of different policies for achieving a particular objective. This type of question is often in the form:

> To what extent is **fiscal** or **monetary** or **DSP** or **SSP** the most effective way of **controlling inflation or unemployment** or **achieving growth**?

Irrespective of the variations, any such questions are basically the same and the major part of your answer will be the same for all of them.

From the section on objectives you will notice that for each of inflation, unemployment and growth there are two types and conveniently there are two policies DSP and SSP. It is the case that for each type or cause one of the policies is likely to be more effective as follows:

Inflation

- Demand pull inflation – DSP
- Cost push inflation – SSP

Unemployment

- Equilibrium unemployment – SSP
- Disequilibrium unemployment –DSP

Growth

- Actual growth – DSP
- Potential or long term growth – SSP

The logic behind this is simply that if the type or cause is on the demand side of the economy then the most direct cure is DSP and if the cause is on the supply side then SSP is more appropriate. For example, since equilibrium unemployment such as structural is part of the natural rate that is consistent with Y_f, it can only be reduced by shifting LRAS to the right. The best way to do this is with SSP. Increasing AD will not have any direct impact on this type of unemployment. Similarly, if the unemployment is cyclical or demand deficient, then it can only be effectively reduced with a DSP that shifts AD towards Y_f. Using a SSP would not be effective as it would simply shift LRAS to the right which would actually increase the deflationary gap.

To summarise:

- **DSP** is effective for reducing:
    - Cyclical unemployment
    - Demand pull inflation
    - And for promoting actual growth
- **SSP** is effective for reducing
    - Cost push inflation
    - Equilibrium unemployment
    - And promoting potential or long term growth

Hopefully this will make answering part (b) macro questions easier and your answer to a question such as: *Using real world examples, evaluate the effectiveness of SSP as a way of reducing unemployment* would include the following sentence, after your definitions of SSP and unemployment:

> The effectiveness of SSP in reducing unemployment will depend on the type of unemployment that the country is facing; if it is equilibrium unemployment such as structural, SSP can be effective but if the unemployment is cyclical then a DSP would be required.

Then you would go on to explain using appropriate diagrams.

9.8   Consequences of failing to achieve the objectives

This section covers the final '**C**' and examines why inflation, unemployment and unequal distribution of income are considered to be a problem. With growth the issue is a bit different as it involves assessments of living standards and environmental implications associated with growth.

Inflation

Since the experience of high inflation during the 1970s and 80s initiated by the OPEC oil price rises, and the ascendancy of the neoclassical school of economics popularised by free market monetarists such as M. Friedman, control of inflation became the prime objective of government policy. The fear of inflation resulting from past experiences has survived into the 21st century despite the fact that no major economy has experienced any inflation problems in over two decades. In fact deflation which is the opposite of inflation has been a bigger problem and threat especially in Japan.

When assessing the potential problems associated with inflation it is necessary to clearly distinguish between hyper-inflation such as that experienced by Germany during the 1930s or Venezuela currently and mild inflation of around 3–5%. Failure to do this leads to an exaggeration of the potential problems that inflation can cause but despite this difference, German finance ministers and Central Bankers still retain an almost paranoiac fear of inflation which has influenced the ECB's monetary policy.

The main reasons why control of inflation is recommended is because it:

An alternative theory suggests that inflation might actually cause targeted saving to increase

- Reduces business and consumer confidence by increasing uncertainty
- Redistributes income less equally
- May have a negative effect on savings
- Negatively affects the creditor/debtor relationship
- Negatively affects the export competitiveness of the country
- Reduces the real incomes of groups who are less able to secure compensatory increases in their incomes
- Reduces the accuracy of the signaling function of the price mechanism
- Increases menu costs
- Increases shoe-leather (search) costs

The last three are not significant and the effect on the debtor/creditor relationship depends on how the real interest rate changes, while the effect on export competitiveness depends on the likely changes to the exchange rate.

Overall, a mild inflation as a result of rising AD is unlikely to generate significant problems unless it creates expectations of higher inflation that will make it ever more difficult to bring under control.

Unemployment

With the ascendancy of the neoclassical viewpoint control of inflation was prioritised over control of unemployment, partly due to the neoclassical belief that if uncontrolled, inflation will destroy business confidence leading to increased unemployment in the long run. Since the 2008 financial crisis, the absence of any significant inflationary pressures in developed economies has led to greater concern with the problem of unemployment and government policy has become more pro-active with regard to addressing the problem of recession and unemployment.

The main problems associated with unemployment are:

- Loss of potential output as the economy is producing within its PPC
- Loss of tax revenues to the government
- Increased spending on unemployment benefits and welfare
- Increased poverty and hardship for the families of the unemployed
- Possible increase in social problems such as alcoholism and crime
- Loss of skills by the long term unemployed
- Loss of self-esteem for the unemployed

For some reason it is assumed that people wear out their shoes while searching for lower prices when faced with inflation but when the unemployed go looking for work they are barefoot. Another anomaly is that although increased cost of pensions is identified as a problem associated with an aging population it is not linked to unemployment which reduces the national insurance contributions that go towards pensions.

Growth

Achieving a high and sustained rate of economic growth has traditionally been a major policy objective and governments are often judged on their growth records. However, increasingly growth is being linked to sustainability due to the negative impact it can have on the environment and climate change. There is serious questioning of whether the increase in living standards achieved by increased consumption of goods compensates for the degradation of the environment that is involved. Smog-laden cities found in many countries including India and China are the result of rapid industrial growth that has allowed more people to own cars, but are these car owners enjoying a higher standard of living than the previous generations who cycled or walked in a clean atmosphere? The link between growth and economic well-being is one that is important for the current syllabus and requires the ability to apply micro concepts of market failure to macro-economic objectives as well as interdependence through international trade.

Equity

With respect to the policy issues regarding equity there is the need to consider the conflict between efficiency and greater equality of income distribution. The policies that are generally considered to be necessary to achieve a more equal distribution of income are:

- Increasing progressive direct taxes relative to regressive indirect taxes
- Increasing minimum wages and welfare payments
- Providing more assistance to low income households

These policies however, are considered to be anti-supply side because they decrease the incentive to work and find employment. In addition, high marginal rates of income tax are thought to have a disincentive effect on work and effort while increasing taxes on company profits are thought to make firms less willing to invest and increase production. These connections are quite complex and subject to various opinions so that questions relating to evaluating policies to achieve greater equity are difficult.

Evaluation of DSP and SSP

Paper 1 part (b) questions are likely to require an evaluation or discussion of how effective a particular policy is likely to be. As well as the points identified in section 9.6, the following should also be considered:

- Time lags – or how quickly the policy will work. Probably the quickest are monetary policy which takes 6–9 months followed by tax changes. SSP such as spending on infrastructure will have the longest lags as will the same policies if described as fiscal.

- The possible crowding out effect that results from an expansionary fiscal policy. This is claimed to occur as a result of the borrowing that is necessitated by the fiscal expansion since G > T. This borrowing is supposed to cause interest rates to increase which will choke off the effects of the fiscal expansion. With respect to real world examples there appears to be no evidence of this actually happening. Since 2008 the world's major economies have experienced historically high budget deficits and borrowing requirements while over the same period these economies have experienced historically low interest rates.

- Monetary policy has a downward limit when interest rates are at or close to zero.

- Monetary policy via changes in interest rates will also affect the exchange rate of the currency.

- If using the Keynesian AS the effectiveness of DSP will depend on the slope of AS.

- If using the Keynesian model the effect of any fiscal policy will be enhanced by the multiplier process. The multiplier (K) works through the circular flow to generate a greater change in Income than any initial change in an injection (I, G or X).

  For example, assume that the government increases its spending on road building by $10 bn. This will lead to an increase in income of more than $10bn because some of the additional income will be spent and received as additional income and so on. The final change in income will depend on the proportion of any additional income that is spent on consumption (this is the **marginal propensity to consume** or MPC). If the MPC = 0.5 it means that the $10bn spent on road building will generate additional spending of $5bn which in turn will generate additional spending of $2.5 bn and so on. The final increase in income will be $20 bn. A numerical value for the multiplier can be calculated as:

$$K = \frac{1}{1 - MPC} \quad \text{or} \quad \frac{1}{MPW} \quad \text{(marginal propensity to withdraw)}$$

  Note that MPW is made up of the **marginal propensity to save** (MPS) the **marginal propensity to tax** (MPT) and the **marginal propensity to import** (MPM).

$$MPC + MPW = 1$$

- A major evaluation point will always be the conflict of policy objectives. For DSP this conflict is mainly between inflation and unemployment since the policy necessary for reducing one will lead to an increase in the other. This inverse relationship can be shown with a Keynesian AD/AS model or alternatively with a short run Phillips curve diagram as shown in Figure 9.11.

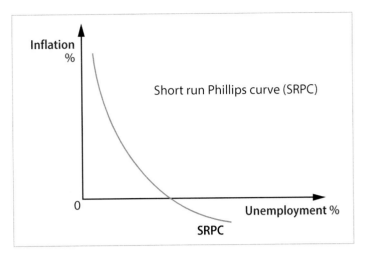

Figure 9.11: **Phillips curve**

The Phillips curve was originally constructed to show a historical statistical relationship between unemployment and the rate of change in money wages based on data for the UK economy 1863–1957. After the supply shocks of the 1970s this relationship was said to have broken down and now the traditional Phillips curve shown in Figure 9.11 is depicted as a short run relationship between inflation and unemployment. In the long run the Phillips curve is considered to be vertical at the natural rate of unemployment which corresponds to the vertical LRAS at the full employment level of income.

This conflict between inflation and unemployment is completely avoided with SSP because any successful SSP that shifts LRAS to the right will simultaneously lead to a decrease in inflation and unemployment as well as promoting potential growth and greater export competitiveness. This constitutes a major advantage of SSP compared to DSP. However, SSP also has a conflict with equality in the distribution of income.

- SSP are also very unpopular with workers and are often resisted with demonstrations and strikes by workers. Whenever the French government attempts to introduce supply side labour market reforms it usually leads to rioting and demonstrations such as with the recent 'Gilets Jaunes' movement.

Chapter 10: The Global Economy

10.1 The gains from trade

Increased international trade over the past 50 years has been the driving force behind the process of globalisation and is attributed partly to greater liberalisation of trade but mainly to the containerisation of sea transportation via ever larger vessels. The value of world trade increased from $318 bn in 1970 to over $19 trn in 2019 and this dramatic rise suggests that there are significant benefits to countries from trade.

The gains from trade are mainly the result of countries specializing in the production of those goods which they can produce most efficiently rather than trying to produce all goods themselves. This gain is expressed through the principle of **comparative advantage** which a country has when it can produce a good at a lower **opportunity cost** than another country. If all countries specialise in accordance with their comparative advantage and trade, the total volume of goods produced will be larger than if countries were self-sufficient. This principle applies even if a country is more efficient at producing all goods which is described as an absolute advantage. The following examples illustrate the gains from comparative rather than absolute advantage.

	CARS	COMPUTERS
Country A	50	200
Country B	25	50

Country A has an absolute advantage in the production of both cars and computers but it has a comparative advantage in computers. It is twice as efficient as country B in producing cars but four times more efficient in producing computers. The opportunity cost of 1 car in A is 4 computers while in B it is 2 computers and the opportunity cost of 1 computer in A is ¼ of a car while in B it is ½ of a car. A has the lower opportunity cost in computers and B in cars so A should specialise in computer production and B in car production and trade with each other. With an exchange rate of 1 car for 3 computers both countries will benefit from trade. With trade, country A gives up 1 car and receives 3 computers whereas domestically for 1 car it could only receive 2 computers. Country B gives up 3 computers and receives 1 car whereas domestically it would have to give up 4 computers to have 1 car.

As long as the cost of transporting the goods between A and B is not greater than the difference in opportunity costs, both countries will benefit from trade.

Comparative and absolute advantage can also be shown diagrammatically as in Figure 10.1.

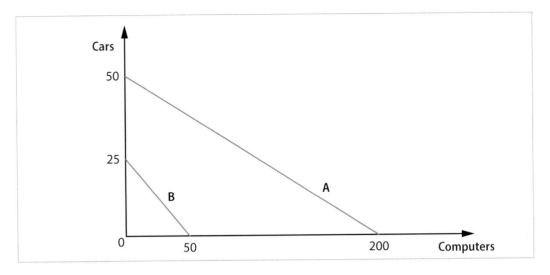

Figure 10.1: **Comparative and absolute advantage**

The difference in comparative advantage between country A and B is indicated by the slope of the PPC for each country which for simplicity are always shown as straight lines rather than curves. In addition to the advantages from specialising and trading in accordance with comparative advantage there are other benefits to be gained as follows:

- Larger production volumes can lead to economies of scale and long run cost benefits
- Expertise is developed from specialising e.g. Switzerland in watches, Scotland in whisky, France in wine
- Countries are encouraged to cooperate with each other
- Consumers are able to have a wider choice of products
- More competition will stimulate efficiency and lower prices
- Benefits of globalisation

There are however, some potential costs involved such as:

- Over specialisation can lead to a lack of diversity in production that exposes the country to risks
- It can lead to overdependence on imports and supply chains (this problem was recently exposed during the pandemic when trade was interrupted and many industries that relied on imports could not function)
- Difficulties in maintaining environmental and health standards and responsible employment conditions
- Costs of globalisation such as loss of cultural identity and exposure of small producers to multinational giant corporations

10.2 Restrictions on the freedom of trade: Protection

Despite the many benefits from free trade it may seem surprising why so many countries choose to limit the freedom of trade with a variety of protectionist policies. Any restriction to free trade is known as protection and there are several reasons used to justify such actions. Whether protection can be justified economically will depend on the particular case but the general consensus of economists is that the benefits of free trade outweigh the benefits of protection, at least in the long run. The popularity of protectionism has more to do with visibility and perceptions than sound economics.

The main arguments in favour of protectionism are:

- **To protect domestic output and employment**: This is a popular argument and was used by President Trump to justify the imposition of tariffs on imported steel and aluminium. The benefits to domestic steel workers are highly visible but the costs from inefficient use of resources and increased production costs to firms that use steel are possibly much higher than these benefits but they are much less visible. In the long run these tariffs are likely to lead to more job losses than those jobs that are saved in the protected industries and the argument is considered to be unjustified by most economists.

- **To help infant industries to become established**: This argument could be justified for a less economically developed country (LEDC) that is attempting to diversify its economy by promoting some manufacturing such as textiles but is unlikely to be valid for a developed economy which already has a sophisticated manufacturing sector. Either way it can only be justified for a limited period.

- **To improve a balance of payments deficit**: At best this can only be a temporary and artificial solution since it in no way tackles the cause of the problem (see later section).

- **To prevent dumping**: Dumping refers to selling goods in foreign markets at prices below cost as a result of subsidies or undervalued currencies. E.g. if a country gives a 10% subsidy to exports of washing machines the importing country is justified in imposing a 10% tariff on them. This actually re-establishes the correct prices that reflect comparative advantage. The problem is that accusations of dumping are often made without any factual basis in order to provide a justification. For example, the Trump administration frequently used this accusation to justify tariffs on Chinese goods and accused China of manipulating its currency, claims that were sometimes considered to be false.

- **For health and safety**: There is clearly some justification in restricting trade in dangerous materials like toxic chemicals and unhealthy food products.

- **For strategic reasons**: This is a potentially justified argument when a degree of self-sufficiency is desirable in strategically important products for national defense purposes, but it tends to be exaggerated as a justification. For example the USA recently tried to justify imposing tariffs on steel imports from Canada for strategic reasons, as if there would ever be a military threat to the USA from Canada.

- **For revenue purposes**: This could be justified for a LEDC which has few efficient sources of revenue but cannot be justified for a developed country which will have a more effective system of taxation.

- **To reduce the negative effects of further globalisation and the carbon footprint of long distance trade**: This is an increasingly important consideration and there is some justification for using more locally sourced products rather than possibly cheaper imports.

- **To reflect a more realistic picture of world trade** than that which is presented by the unrealistic assumptions regarding comparative advantage and the fact that it can change rapidly and become a disruptive element. Factors of production are not perfectly mobile and comparative advantage can change more quickly than the reallocation of resources that it requires.

▶ **To reduce the carbon footprint associated with long distance trade routes** and encourage more eco-friendly reliance on local produce.

10.3 Types of protection

Tariffs

This is the most popular protectionist measure and represents a tax on imports which has the effect of shifting the world supply of a product upwards by the amount of the tariff leading to an increase in price and reduction in quantity imported and consumed domestically. The effects of a tariff are shown in Figure 10.2.

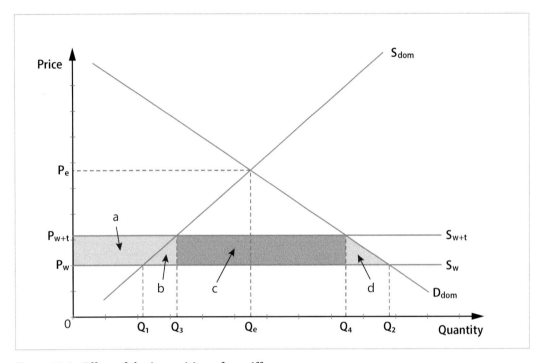

Figure 10.2: **Effect of the imposition of a tariff**

Without trade Q_e would be produced and consumed domestically at price P_e. With free trade and a world supply at S_w the price would be P_w and domestic consumption would increase to Q_2 while domestic production would fall to Q_1. The imposition of a tariff will shift the world supply to P_{w+t} and domestic consumption will now fall to Q_4 while domestic production increases to Q_3. In total consumers will lose consumer surplus equal to the combined area a+b+c+d. Area a will be transferred to producers and area c will be transferred to the government as additional revenue. Areas b and d however are not gained by anyone and represent a deadweight efficiency loss to the economy.

In addition to this net welfare loss there are other likely costs such as the possibility of retaliation by the foreign exporting countries. This is what happened in 2018 when the Trump administration increased tariffs on a range of imports from China. In retaliation, China imposed tariffs on US goods and restricted the import of soya beans from America. This necessitated the US government paying soya bean farmers billions of dollars in compensation. Tariffs on a wide range of goods will increase production costs for domestic firms and can cause inflationary pressures to build up while the higher prices might lead to a fall in domestic demand for local products.

Finally, it can be argued that tariffs, by reducing competition, encourage domestic firms to be inefficient leading to a further misallocation of resources.

The example of US tariffs on imported washing machines to protect the domestic producer Whirlpool provides a useful insight into how tariffs can be counterproductive.

Just before leaving office President Trump extended the tariffs on imported washing machines which initially benefitted Whirlpool as the main US producer. The protection that Whirlpool had managed to secure over the years was against imported machines from S. Korea manufactured by Samsung and LG. in response the Korean companies switched their exports to their Chinese factories and when tariffs were imposed on these they switched again to their factories in Thailand and Vietnam. Whirlpool managed to secure tariffs on these imports as well which enabled them to increase their domestic sales to the detriment of US consumers who were now paying over 12% more for washing machines.

After this latest extension of tariffs Samsung and LG decided to open factories in the USA so now Whirlpool faces direct competition in the domestic market from more efficient and productive producers using the latest technology.

Exactly what benefits were gained by Whirlpool and the US economy in the long run is difficult to assess but it is quite likely that Whirlpool will steadily lose market share to the new competitors as the absence of competition due to protection over the past decade has reduced incentives to cut costs and operate efficiently.

Without tariff protection, US consumers would have benefitted from cheaper washing machines and increased choice, while US companies would have been forced to become more efficient in order to compete.

It should also be noted that one reason for Whirlpool's lack of competitiveness could be due to the US imposing tariffs on imported steel and aluminium which are used in the manufacture of washing machines

Quotas

These have a similar effect as tariffs in reducing imports but do not provide revenue to the government. They represent limits to the quantity or volume of imports that are allowed leading to an increase in price and reduction in quantity as shown in Figure 10.3.

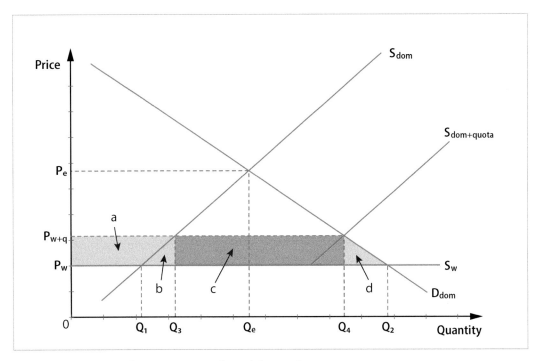

Figure 10.3: **Impact of quotas on supply and demand**

The quota will shift the domestic supply to the right by the amount of the quota leading to an increase in price to P_{w+q} and a decrease in domestic consumption to Q_4. Again, domestic producers of the good benefit at the expense of domestic consumers and economic efficiency.

Subsidies

These provide an artificial cost benefit to exporters who are able to gain an artificial comparative advantage in the production of the good. It will lead to unfair competition from exporters and possibly dumping which could be used as a means of driving foreign producers out of business. Diagrammatically it can be represented with a familiar subsidy diagram with the addition of a world supply.

Bureaucratic controls

These can be used to make trade difficult by delaying imports etc and are mainly applied when countries have free trade agreements that prevent official methods of protection.

10.4 Trading Blocs

These are various trading arrangements made between countries to facilitate freer trade. They can be in the form of:

▶   **bilateral or multilateral preferential trade agreements** where trading preference is given to the members;

▶   **a free trade area** which establishes free trade between members and individual arrangements with non-members;

▶   **a customs union** which is as above but with a common external tariff on non-members;

▶ **a common market** which is as above but with additional free movement of labour and capital between members; or

▶ **a monetary union** which is as above but with a common currency, as with the Eurozone members of the EU which use the euro and monetary policy is set by the European Central Bank (ECB).

Members of trading blocs benefit from trade creation through free trade between members but may suffer as a result of trade diversion through the tariff on non-members. There will therefore be a mix of free trade benefits together with some costs of protection and the net benefits for countries are difficult to assess sometimes.

In 2016 the UK voted to leave the EU supposedly in order to secure greater sovereignty and economic benefits by being able to secure trade deals with non EU member countries. Since its departure, however, very few of these 'benefits' have been realised and there are strong indications that the loss of trade with the EU is far greater than any new trade deals. A recent report (June 2021) indicates that UK food and drink exports to the EU fell by 2 billion pounds in the first quarter of 2021. In addition, as a single country the UK has much less bargaining power in international markets than the EU and restrictions on the free movement of workers from the EU has led to serious labour shortages in many key industries such as health care, hospitality and farming. A recent UK trade deal signed with Australia will allow imports of cheap beef that might benefit UK consumers but it is feared will lead to bankruptcy for some UK cattle farmers.

10.5 Exchange Rates (ER)

The ER of a country's currency is the price of that currency in terms of another currency. In a free market, the exchange rate like any other price will be determined by supply and demand as shown in Figure 10.4 where the exchange rate for the $ is established at ER.

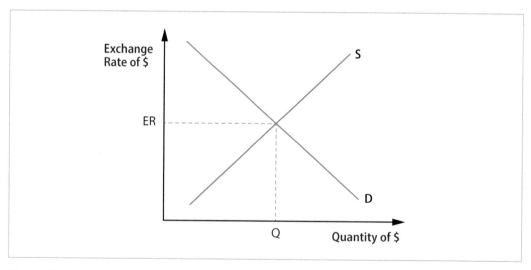

Figure 10.4: **Determination of equilibrium exchange rate**

A major source of the demand for a currency is the demand for the country's exports while the supply of a currency reflects the demand for imports. Once the equilibrium exchange rate has been established at ER it will change in response to any change in exports or imports or any other factor that could cause the supply or demand for the currency to shift such as:

- changes in interest rates ;
- speculative currency trading;
- Foreign Direct Investment (FDI) flows;
- Central Bank intervention.

For example, if the US Federal Reserve increases interest rates it means that US financial assets now have a higher return and are more attractive so funds will flow into the US meaning that the demand for dollars will increase and the dollar will appreciate (increase). Similarly if international speculators and traders anticipate changes they will buy or sell a currency accordingly causing exchange rates to change. A country's Central Bank can also directly influence the exchange rate of its currency by buying or selling its currency on the foreign exchange market.

A notable example of speculation inspired exchange rate changes occurred with the Brexit referendum in 2016. On the day of the referendum speculators predicted a 'remain' vote and the pound appreciated significantly, however the following day when the 'leave' majority was announced the pound depreciated by over 20%.

10.6 The effects of exchange rate changes

The ER of a country's currency is one of the most important prices in an economy as it affects the prices of exports and imports which will in turn affect the level of AD as well as SRAS. The ER is both affected by the macro economy and affects the macro economy. The following scenario identifies some of the major implications of a change in the ER.

An increase in the ER leads to an increase in the price of exports and a decrease in the price of imports – this in turn leads to a decrease in the volume of exports and an increase in the volume of imports – if the demand for exports and imports is >1 there will be a decrease in export revenues and an increase in spending on imports – this will then lead to a deficit in trade in goods and services (X < M) and then to a decrease in AD – at the same time the decrease in import prices could be significant for a country that imports oil and raw materials. In this case there would be a decrease in costs of production causing the SRAS to shift to the right which would have a beneficial effect on decreasing inflation and stimulating output.

> This elasticity assumption relates to the Marshall-Lerner condition that states that a depreciation of a currency will only lead to an improvement in X – M if the combined elasticities of demand for imports and exports is >1.

In the above scenario if the Marshall-Lerner condition was not met the increase in the ER would have the opposite effect on X – M and subsequently on AD. Whenever discussing the possible effects of changes in the ER on the economy it is always important to make an elasticities assumption.

In theory a floating ER system in which the ER is determined by market forces operating freely in the foreign exchange market, will guarantee equilibrium in a country's trade because a deficit will cause the ER to depreciate and a surplus will cause it to appreciate. These ER changes will lead to changes in X and M which will restore equilibrium. For this to happen however, requires that trade flows adjust quickly to ER changes and that the Marshall-Lerner condition is met. If it is not then deficits or surpluses will get larger before they recover and the process could take a relatively long time. This can give rise to what is known as the J-curve effect. This effect is frequently observed when a country's trade deficit causes a depreciation of the ER and as a result the deficit actually increases. This is because trade flows take 6–9 months to adjust to price changes which mean that for this period the Marshall-Lerner condition is not satisfied.

There are some important links between the macro economy and a country's trade which are seldom fully explored. There is a tendency for macro and trade to be separated with only some basic links examined such as that between ERs and AD and possibly SRAS.

There are however, some more complicated but important links that are often overlooked.

One of these is the link between interest rates and the ER which has wider implications than are often considered.

Specifically, the fact that an increase in interest rates represents an example of monetary policy aimed at decreasing inflation.

As seen in the scenario outlined above an increase in the ER will assist the interest rate policy in reducing demand pull inflation as it will lead to a further decrease in AD. In addition to this there is the possibility that the decrease in import prices will cause the SRAS to increase which will also decrease cost push inflationary pressures. This adds an important dimension to the potential effectiveness of interest rate policy as an means of tackling inflation as it has an impact on both demand pull and cost push. It also provides a strong link between macro and trade and emphasises the need to study economics as an integrated whole rather than putting each syllabus section into separate boxes.

10.7 Alternative ER systems

The world's major currencies are traded freely in the foreign exchange market but some currencies are not traded freely or are subject to government influence. The opposite extreme of freely floating ERs is a system of fixed ERs whereby the ERs are maintained at a pre-determined fixed parity. For example, Saudi Arabia, Qatar, UAE, Panama, Hong Kong and Belize have their currencies pegged against the US dollar. The aim is to create a greater degree of stability because without this fixing there would be a high degree of ER volatility which could be damaging for business confidence.

In order to maintain fixed parities countries have to be able and willing to intervene in the foreign exchange market as necessary or to be able to control capital flows or influence them with interest rate changes. For small economies this is possible but for a major currency the degree of intervention that would be necessary would be prohibitive.

An alternative that some countries favour is to allow the ER to be determined freely but to intervene sporadically in order to influence the ER if necessary. This is known as a system of managed ERs. An example of this type of intervention is by the Swiss Central Bank which sometimes enters the foreign exchange market to sell Swiss Francs in order to prevent an appreciation when there is speculative buying of the currency due to its status as a safe haven.

Changes in the ER are described differently depending on the ER system in operation. Under floating ERs a decrease is a **depreciation** and an increase is an **appreciation** while under fixed ERs the same movements are described as **devaluation** and **revaluation**.

Given the huge volume of currency trading (over $6 trillion daily in 2020) it would be practically impossible for major currencies to operate fixed ERs so even if it was thought to be desirable in the interests of stability and certainty it would not be feasible. In the long run floating ERs are more conducive to responsible trade and macro policies though their ability to accurately reflect purchasing power and to correct trade imbalances is less effective than theory suggests.

Economic theory predicts that in a free foreign exchange market, ERs will adjust so that they reflect purchasing parities but although there is long term tendency for this to occur in practice many currencies remain under or overvalued for relatively long periods. *The Economist* frequently publishes a 'Big Mac' index which shows which currencies are over or undervalued and by how much.

10.8 Balance of Payments

This is a record of the total value of transactions which give rise to currency flows between one country and the rest of the world. It consists of 3 sections:

- the current account;
- the capital account;
- the financial account.

The **current account** is the most important as it reflects the trading performance of the country. It includes the balance of trade in goods and services together with income flows and transfers. It broadly corresponds to the (X – M) component of AD. If X > M there is a current account **surplus** and if X < M there is a current account **deficit**.

The capital account includes capital transfers and transactions in non-produced and non-financial assets. The balance of the current and capital accounts will always be balanced by the financial account which includes FDI, portfolio investments, reserves and official borrowing. If the balance on current account is –$10 billion and on capital account –$2 billion the financial account will be +$12 billion.

10.9 Current Account disequilibria

In addition to the macro economic objectives of inflation, unemployment, growth and equity governments are also concerned to maintain a reasonable balance in their current account. A plus or minus of less than 2% of GDP is generally acceptable but anything above this margin can be seen as a problem if persistent and growing. Popular perceptions, often reinforced by the media, support the mistaken belief that a surplus is good and only a deficit is bad. From a world viewpoint this is illogical as they are the same thing since a deficit in one country has to be matched by a surplus in another country. Possibly a deficit is a more urgent problem than a surplus but the best situation for the future of world trade is for all countries to have neither large persistent deficits nor surpluses. For Germany and the Netherlands to maintain their current account surpluses of 6.8% and 7.2% of GDP, requires that some other countries like Greece must have a deficit. This means that Germany is consuming less than it produces while Greece is consuming more than it produces so this could mean that Greece is benefitting more than Germany. Of course in the long run Greece will have to reduce its deficit or not be able to repay its loans and will have to stop buying so many goods from Germany. If this happens Germany will lose an export market and its economy that is geared to exports will suffer so there is a strong possibility that the surplus countries will be forced to bail out the deficit countries so that trading can continue as occurred with the Greek debt crisis 2010–2016. If surplus countries spent their surpluses so that deficit countries had smaller deficits the world trade climate would be much more conducive to continuous mutual growth and benefits.

10.10 **How to correct a current account deficit**

The IB expects students to be aware that any trade imbalance is potentially a problem but the majority of questions will be directed to curing deficit problems rather than surplus problems.

For a country that has a large and persistent deficit there 3 policy approaches that can be followed in order to correct the deficit:

- Expenditure switching
- Expenditure reducing
- SSP

Expenditure switching policies aim to switch spending from imports to domestic produce and to encourage spending on exports. This could be achieved by depreciating the exchange rate to make exports more competitive and imports less competitive. Alternatively protectionist policies could be imposed as was done by the Trump administration but such policies tend to be counterproductive in the long run.

Expenditure reducing policies refer to contractionary DSP which aim to reduce level of domestic demand which in turn will reduce the demand for imports since a proportion of income will be always be spent on imports.

The problem with these policies is that they will conflict with the other economic objectives which is why correcting current account deficits is often given a low priority by governments. In theory with freely floating ERs such deficits should be self-correcting through ER changes but this is not always the case due to elasticities, time lags and other complications.

The third approach through SSP potentially avoids some of these problems and can lead to a more efficient and competitive trade sector for the country but as noted they are very difficult to implement and can conflict with the objective of equity.

In order to correct a surplus the opposite expenditure policies would be recommended such as appreciating the currency and increasing AD. Reverse SSP would not be recommended.

10.11 **Some additional points**

There are several misconceptions relating to trade and ERs and perceptions can be misleading. One problem is with the terminology that is used to describe currencies and ER changes. For example, strong and weak are applied to currencies when they appreciate and depreciate. These are emotive terms that imply good and bad. Current account surpluses are described in complimentary terms while deficits are usually presented unfavourably. These descriptions should not be taken literally and a balanced opinion of the actual desirability of a 'strong' currency or a 'surging surplus' should be maintained. Whether strong or weak is good or bad depends exclusively on the circumstances involved.

10.12 Development Economics

This section of the syllabus is concerned with the reasons that economic development is uneven and what can be done to promote greater and more equitable development in LEDCs. In the past the emphasis for comparisons between countries was on growth and economic welfare but nowadays the emphasis is more on wider measures and indicators of social welfare and development in addition to economic measures. A basic measure of development and well-being is the Human Development Index (HDI) which is a composite that includes income per capita, health and education as indicated by life expectancy and adult literacy and years of schooling. There is increasing concern for sustainable development that does not involve sacrificing the welfare of future generations and factors such as gender equality, empowerment and quality of life are important considerations that various indices try to measure such as the Happy Planet Index.

Economic growth and income are very important determinants of well-being but overall development needs to be seen as a multidimensional concept. For example, a country can achieve economic growth as a result of exploiting mineral deposits or developing a textile industry but if this leads to environmental destruction or the employment of children who would otherwise have attended school, it will be growth at the expense of development.

10.13 Barriers to development

LEDCs share many common features and barriers to development which have proven to be difficult to overcome. Recent studies have begun to question some of the traditional policies that have been advocated for achieving growth and development such as the benefits of aid and the role of SSP policies such as privatisation. Development issues are quite complex and solutions are complicated and cannot be easily incorporated into IB economics so the following treatment will follow traditional mainstream theory and interpretations.

Common barriers include:

▶   **Artificial geographical boundaries**: this problem is faced by many African countries that were colonised and created as artificial countries that comprised many ethnic and culturally diverse elements so that on gaining independence there was a lack of linguistic, ethnic and cultural unity that made economic and political harmony difficult to achieve. Many such countries are still afflicted by civil wars and conflicts.

▶   **Dependence on a narrow range of primary commodities**: this means that there is a lack of diversity in economic activities and overdependence on production and export of low value products with volatile prices. For example, the Ivory Coast depends heavily on cocoa and the fortunes of the economy fluctuate in accordance with the world cocoa price. A similar problem is faced by Nigeria which depends for 90% of its export revenues on Oil.

▶ **Poverty and its perpetuation through the poverty cycle:**

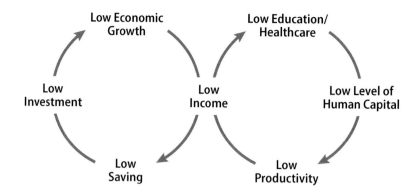

In order to break out of the cycle at least one of the links needs to be broken. Each of the links in the cycle represents a barrier to growth and development.

▶ **Lack of infrastructure** that hinders transportation, communications, and access to amenities.

▶ **High levels of debt** that act as a burden on domestic resources as a large % of GDP has to be devoted to interest payments.

▶ **High levels of income and gender inequality.**

▶ **Hypocritical trade policies pursued by the EU and the USA** which provide subsidies to domestic cotton and sugar producers so that African producers are squeezed out of the market. In addition trade restrictions on LEDCs often prevent them from developing secondary industries to process their raw materials and gain more value added. For example, Ethiopia exports high quality coffee beans but could gain much higher revenue if it was able to sell packaged coffee products.

In addition to these factors many LEDCs are being disproportionately impacted by global crises such as climate change and related extreme conditions of drought and the recent plague of locusts that destroyed crops in East Africa. The current pandemic is also taking a heavy toll on lives in Sub Saharan Africa (SSA) and creating a huge strain on already inadequate health services and travel restrictions have greatly reduced revenues from tourism. It will take these countries much longer to recover than in the developed countries as their access to Covid-19 vaccines is still quite limited.

10.14 Strategies to promote economic growth and development

Aid

The fact that so many SSA countries remain in a critical state of underdevelopment with high levels of both absolute poverty (income < $1.9 a day) and relative poverty (income < 50% of the average) despite having received $ billions in aid might suggest that new approaches are needed. This is in fact forcefully argued by Dambisa Moyo in her book *Dead Aid* where she claims that even well intentioned aid tends to be counterproductive as it creates dependence and removes incentives. For example, she cites the case of providing free mosquito nets to African villages to reduce the spread of malaria. What could be bad about this? Well it means that local producers of nets cannot sell them and are forced out of business leading to local unemployment. A similar situation arises with the distribution of free food as part of a famine relief program. This does provide an important assistance to many poor families but it also means that local farmers are unable to sell any of their produce so they will not be able to buy seeds for planting crops in the next season and the famine will carry over into next year. The way that aid is disbursed is clearly very important and in the above cases a more sensible policy would be first to buy up all the local produce and then add this to the free products to be distributed.

In addition, it is often the case that the aid is bilateral from one government to another rather than for a specific development project. This can lead to the misappropriation of the aid by the officials ending up in foreign bank accounts. Aid is often conditional or tied to requirements to buy from the donor country and the beneficiary is the donor rather than the recipient. Such aid leads to political influence by donor countries that might use the aid as leverage to secure votes and support on international bodies such as the UN. Aid is seldom completely altruistic and donors expect some payback.

Trade

This partial reassessment of the role of aid in promoting development has inspired the mantra 'Trade not Aid' implying that what LEDCs need in order to achieve growth and development is a free market economy and to engage in free trade with the rest of the world. Towards this end various international bodies such as the International Monetary Fund (IMF) and the World Bank supported the implementation of structural adjustment programs incorporating market oriented SSP as a prerequisite for securing loans and assistance. The Nobel laureate economist formerly with the World Bank, J. Stiglitz, has been a forceful critic of this policy and blames it for causing more problems than it solved. Only recently has the IMF reassessed its austerity policy in the light of the devastating effect that these had on the Greek economy when it granted a bailout package in 2012–16.

Encouraging LEDCs to trade freely is also hypocritical as the developed world consistently restricts the ability of LEDCs to compete freely in world markets with their farm subsidies and import restrictions. The treatment of LEDCs is also very inconsistent with respect to trade policies, for example, Kenya was encouraged to diversify its agriculture and produce vegetables such as mange tout and flowers for export. Kenyan farmers duly adapted their production only for the EU to decide that importing these from Kenya had too high a carbon footprint and that it was better to buy these goods from wealthy farmers in the Netherlands. Many

Many of you will have heard the 'wise' saying that if you give a man a fish you feed him for one day but if you teach a man to fish you feed him for life.

I have a more cynical version of the second part which is: 'if you teach a man to fish you have a customer for life who will need to buy boats, fishing nets etc. etc.'

When the EU 'taught' Somalians to fish they proved to be very good at it – so much so that the European fishing industry took advantage of the absence of a strong Somali government that could impose restrictions on fishing, and began trawling off the Somali coast. This had the effect of severely reducing the fish population available for Somali fishermen which left them with boats and little else. Some of these resentful fishermen decided to become 'pirates' and used their boats to capture foreign ships and demand ransom payments. Clearly this is an illegal and dangerous activity, but would it have happened without 'illegal' plundering of Somali fish stocks? Perhaps a new saying is in order:

> *Teach a man to fish and be content to have a customer who will buy boats and fishing gear for life, but if you take a man's fish you might turn him into a pirate.*

SSA countries are able to produce meat at competitive prices but the EU imposes a 26% tariff on African meat.

FDI

The role of FDI in promoting growth and development is a very controversial topic and it is very difficult to assess the overall benefits against the costs. Until recently the majority of FDI in SSA was with respect to mineral extraction by large multinational corporations (MNCs). These MNCs have been accused of plundering the wealth of the countries that they operate in, making huge profits with little economic benefit to the local population while contributing to environmental destruction in the process. For this reason many African governments are attempting to renegotiate mining contracts more favourably and the mining companies are increasingly being forced by public opinion to behave with a greater degree of social responsibility. If this process continues it is possible that a net cost situation for many countries can be converted into a net benefit situation. However, minerals are a non-renewable source of wealth and growth and development based on this is unsustainable. In addition, mining perpetuates the over dependence on volatile primary products which constitutes a major barrier to development. If FDI is to provide sustainable benefits it needs to promote greater diversification in economic activity. This is increasingly being achieved as a result of FDI by Chinese companies which involve the development of manufacturing industries as well as agricultural diversification into higher value products. For example, Chinese FDI in Ethiopia has led to the creation of shoe manufacturing which uses the large available quantities of leather. A country can earn much more from exporting shoes than from exporting leather. Similarly in cotton producing countries like Burkina Faso using the raw cotton to produce textiles is much more profitable than exporting cotton at a depressed world price as a result of US cotton subsidies. Chinese FDI has also stimulated agricultural diversification into products that are exported to China such as soya beans. To facilitate these activities Chinese FDI has also been directed to creating and improving infrastructure such as roads and ports and these projects will benefit the entire economy.

Against these positive benefits however, is the fact that a lot of Chinese FDI relies on Chinese imported labour and few local jobs might be created. In addition, working conditions are often not very good and some Chinese companies have little respect for local culture and the environment.

FDI is very much a double-edged sword generating both costs and benefits. It would be much better for the countries to provide the investment and promote the necessary diversification themselves, but they are not in a position to do this. This means that FDI for all its faults might be the only feasible solution for many LEDCs to break the poverty cycle and diversify their economies. Greater public scrutiny of the way that MNCs operate is gradually creating greater responsibility and accountability so that some companies are beginning to try to improve their image and are providing local amenities, such as schools and health clinics. This should not be at the expense of good working conditions and fair wages however as is often the case in the textile factories in Bangladesh and other Asian countries.

Market or State?

This is a popular question that seeks to explore whether growth and development can be best promoted through the free market or through state intervention.

Many LEDCs are subject to bureaucratic regulations regarding economic enterprises that make setting up and running a business very difficult and costly in bribes that have to be paid to officials. In many countries this system is a way of life and can be viewed as a tax on business. Changing such systems is extremely difficult as there are many vested interests involved but some reduction in regulations is possible and increasingly governments in LEDCs are implementing more market friendly policies to make setting up business easier and encouraging competition. Some market based policies can definitely encourage growth such as deregulation, but the popular SSP of privatisation has not always had benefits in LEDCs. In many cases it has simply replaced state monopolies with private monopolies leading to increased prices and exploitation of consumers while perpetuation corrupt nepotism in the granting of monopoly rights. Like FDI privatisation has had mixed effects on economies sometimes leading to lower prices and sometimes to higher prices. One general negative effect however, as examined by T. Piketty (*Capital and Ideology*, 2019) is that it has tended to foster an increase in income inequality which he considers to be a major barrier to growth and development.

With respect to development, health care and education are two important components together with income. Increased market freedom and competition is likely to best promote economic growth and increased income rather than state intervention, but for health and education the same does not necessarily apply. These merits goods will tend to be underprovided in a market system as they have positive externalities that are not reflected in the market. Therefore, it is unlikely that a free market will ensure adequate provision of health and education and a better solution would be for these merit goods to be provided by the state.

This leads to the conclusion that the growth or economic part of development can best be achieved through the market but the education and health part is best provided by the government as they are typical examples of market failure.

Technology

Increasingly many of the problems faced by LEDCs are being overcome through technological development and in many cases these countries benefit from 'leapfrogging'. For example, when mobile phones were developed they gradually replaced landline phones in developed countries leading to a waste of past investment in the old technology. In many LEDCs there were hardly any landline connections so mobile phones did not replace much but simply provided a new product that became widely accessible. The advent of the mobile phone is possibly the single most important contributor to growth and development in SSA. It provides access to important information such as the price of seeds and fertiliser for farmers and which market to sell their catch for fishermen. Apps have also been developed in Africa which enable users to operate payments and banking services so that there is no need to provide bank branches to remote areas and no need for people to use banks. Mobile phone apps have also been used by doctors to receive instructions from experts so that they have performed lifesaving surgery. Together with the internet and computers, mobile phones have had a huge impact on economic growth and development in SSA and many other LEDCs. As long as a community has access to electricity and the internet it can perform a very wide variety of economic and social activities that were previously impossible. As has been observed worldwide during the recent pandemic, platforms like zoom have facilitated access to schooling through distance learning as well as facilitating working from home.

Charging mobile phones was a problem in remote areas but an enterprising Kenyan worked out a method of charging phones from pedaling a bicycle.

Finally, social media has given many potential entrepreneurs in LEDCs a breakthrough as a means of presenting and promoting their products and services including fashion designers, musicians and artists. This rapid rise of entrepreneurial activity is rapidly transforming the economic climate in SSA.

Other Factors

There are no easy development strategies and each country may have its own unique set of problems. Free trade may be a good policy for countries that have a high degree of diversity but for countries that still rely on a narrow range of primary export products import restrictions to promote import substitution might be more appropriate at least until some diversified production can be established. It should be remembered that the 'Asian Tigers' of South Korea, Hong Kong, Taiwan and Singapore did not go from agriculture to industry overnight. They developed their industrial strength after a period of import substitution and subsequently were able to compete freely in world markets.

In some LEDCs **micro finance** has had a positive effect on development by stimulating the establishment of new businesses, especially by women who constitute a much underutilised resource in many LEDCs. However, micro finance has also been criticised for increasing the debt burdens on poor households as the interest payments on the loans is usually quite high. In addition, some studies have shown that micro finance loans in parts of South Africa have simply enabled the borrowers to set up businesses that compete with existing businesses with no net gain to the community.

A similar situation exists with the well intentioned **fair trade** policy whereby producers of agricultural products and crafts are guaranteed a fair price for their exports so that they are not at the mercy of fluctuating market prices. Many Western retailers such as Starbucks and M&S advertise their commitment to selling fair trade coffee and other products which has prompted some suspicious commentators to wonder who actually benefits most, the producers or the retailers. It has also been argued that by guaranteeing a fair price to producers this policy perpetuates the dependence of countries on a narrow range of agricultural products like coffee, tea or cocoa whereas if faced with market price fluctuations producers would be more likely to diversify into other products.

One policy that has enjoyed relatively high rates of success in poverty reduction is **conditional cash transfers**. These represent direct cash payments to women on condition that they send their children to school and attend health clinics for vaccinations and treatments. These programs have been very successfully employed in Brazil and Mexico and are attracting much attention in development circles though not as yet by the IB.

In all fairness the topic of development is very large and it is not possible for any general course on economics to study it in sufficient depth, nor is it appropriate for a more extensive treatment in a revision guide like this.

My main aim here is to identify and emphasise some of the important issues and to supplement the mainstream topic areas with some up to date insights.

Apart from the poverty cycle, there are no diagrams that are unique to development so all the diagrams that are required are taken from the other parts of the syllabus. Questions on development might be asked for paper 1, but there is a great likelihood of some parts of paper 2 questions to be on development topics. It is unlikely that there will be development questions on paper 3 which will be broadly based on calculations. For paper 2 questions there is likely to be some development data presented for a particular question from which development topics could be tested.

Chapter 11: Additional topics

The topics that have been covered so far have been mainly presented in a form that will be most useful for paper 1 and paper 2 questions that require diagrams, explanations and discussion or evaluation. For paper 3 and a couple of short questions on paper 2 you will also be required to perform some calculations. These are usually quite simple and require an ability to learn some formulas and to press the correct buttons on a calculator. The topic areas where calculations might be required are:

- Opportunity cost from a PPC
- PED/YED/PES
- Tax revenues from the imposition of an indirect tax
- Cost of a subsidy to the government
- Effects of taxes, subsidies and price controls
- Community surplus (consumer + producer surplus)
- Costs, revenues, and profit
- % changes over time
- GDP and GDP per capita
- Real values from nominal values using a deflator
- Growth rates
- CPI/inflation rate
- Unemployment rate
- Multiplier
- Total tax paid by an individual
- Average tax rate
- Real interest rate
- Volumes and values of imports and exports from a trade diagram
- Opportunity cost to identify comparative advantage
- Effects on stakeholders of tariffs, quotas and subsidies
- Exchange rate changes
- Components of the Balance of Payments

A full treatment of the necessary techniques required for answering quantitative (numerical) questions is provided in the companion books in this series written by George Graves published by Peak Study Resources. These comprise a question and answer book for paper 2 and a separate question and answer book for paper 3. In this latter book there will be detailed information regarding how to answer any of the numerical questions and sample questions will be provided together with answers on all the above topics. For this guide I will present two examples of the type of numerical questions that could be asked.

11.1 Numerical questions

EXAMPLE 1

National Income statistics	2019 ($bn)	2020 ($bn)
Consumption	4.2	4.6
Investment	0.4	0.4
Government Spending	2.8	2.9
Exports	1.2	1.4
Imports	1.6	1.7
Net property income from abroad	–0.3	–0.3
Wages and Salaries	3.9	3.9

1. Calculate:

    (a) GDP in 2019 and 2020.   [2 marks]

    (b) GNI in 2019 and 2020.   [2 marks]

2. Calculate the % change in nominal GDP from 2019 to 2020.   [2 marks]

3. If the deflator for 2020 is 103 calculate real GDP for 2020.   [2 marks]

4. Give one possible reason for the increase in imports in 2020.   [1 mark]

5. If this economy has an mps = 0.2 mpt = 0.2 mpm = 0.1 Calculate the value of the multiplier.   [2 marks]

6. As a result of the increase in exports in 2020, calculate the change in National Income that this is likely to generate.   [2 marks]

7. If CPI inflation is 3% in 2020 what would be the CPI for 2019?   [1 mark]

8. If the rate of unemployment was 4% in 2019 would you expect it to be higher or lower in 2020? Give a reason for your answer.   [3 marks]

9. What do you consider to be the most likely cause of the 3% inflation in 2020? Give a reason for your answer.   [3 marks]

Answers

1. (a) GDP = C + I + G + (X – M) = 4.2 + 0.4 + 2.8 – 0.4 = $7 bn (2019)

    (b) 4.6 + 0.4 + 2.9 – 0.3 = $7.6 bn (2020)

2. % Change = 0.6/7 × 100 = 8.57%

3. Real GDP for 2020 = Nominal GDP/deflator × 100 = $7.6/103 × 100 = $7.38 bn

4. The increase in consumption

5. The multiplier = 1/mpw = 1/(0.2 + 0.2 + 0.1) = 1/0.5 = 2

6. Change in exports = + $0.2 bn and the multiplier = 2 so the increase in National Income will be $0.2 bn × 2 = $0.4 bn

7. CPI for 2019 would be 100 (103 – 3)

8. Since overall the components of AD have increased there is likely to be a decrease in unemployment as there will be an increase in real GDP and output assuming that some of the unemployed are cyclically unemployed

9. The most likely cause of the inflation is demand pull since the statistics show an increase in consumer spending possibly as a result of an increase in consumer confidence.

 EXAMPLE 2

The following table shows the income tax rates for different income levels in Argos in $.

Income $	Tax Rate %
0–10,000	0
10,000–20,000	10
20,000–40,000	25
40,000+	50

Don has an income of $26,000.

Mary has an income of $38,000.

Jane has an income of $60,000.

1. Calculate the total amount of income tax paid by Don, Mary and Jane.   [6 marks]

2. Calculate the average tax rate for Don, Mary and Jane.   [3 marks]

3. On the basis of your answer to (2) how would you describe the tax system in Argos?   [2 marks]

In neighbouring Pargos everybody pays 10% tax on all their income.

4. With reference to equity considerations how would you describe the tax system in Pargos compared to Argos?   [4 marks]

5. If Don, Mary and Jane each spend 80% of their disposal income and indirect taxes are introduced at 20% calculate the total amount that each will now pay in taxes in Argos.   [5 marks]

6. Calculate the new average tax rate for Don, Mary and Jane.   [3 marks]

7. Explain whether the tax system in Argos has become more or less progressive?   [2 marks]

Answers

1. Tax paid by Don = 10% of 10,000 + 25% of 6,000 = $1000 + $1,500 = $2,500

   Tax paid by Mary = 10% of 10,000 + 25% of 18,000 = $1000 + $4,500 = $5,500

   Tax paid by Jane = 10% of 10,000 + 25% of 20,000 + 50% of 20,000

   = $1,000 + $5,000 + $10,000 = $16,000

2.   Average Tax Rate (ATR) = Total tax paid/Income × 100

      Don = 2,500/26,000 = 9.61

      Mary = 5,500/38,000 = 14.47

      Jane = 16,000/60,000 = 26.67

3.   The fact that the ART is increasing as income increases is a clear indication that the tax system in Argos is progressive meaning that a higher proportion of tax is paid on higher incomes than on lower incomes.

4.   Equity with respect to taxation refers to fairness and is a normative concept based on personal opinion. Some people would consider the system in Pargos to be fair because it treats everyone the same. However, some people would consider the progressive tax system in Argos to be fairer (more equitable) because the tax burden is higher on those who can afford to pay more and the system leads to a more equal distribution of income.

5.   Disposable income = Income – income tax

      For Don: $26,000 – $2,500 = $23,500

      For Mary: $38,000 – $5,500 = $32,500

      For Jane: $60,000 – $16,000 = $44,000

   Amount spent = 80% of Disposable income

      For Don = $18,800

      For Mary = $26,000

      For Jane = $35,200

   Indirect tax paid = 20% of disposable income

      For Don = $3,760

      For Mary = $5,200

      For Jane = $7,040

   Total tax now paid:

      For Don = $2,500 + $3,760 = $6,260

      For Mary = $ 5,500 + $5,200 = $10,700

      For Jane = $16,000 + $7,040 = $23,040

6.   ATR:

      Don = 6,260/26,000 × 100 = 24.08

      Mary = 10,700/38,000 × 100 = 28.16

      Jane = 23,040/60,000 × 100 = 38.4

7.   The introduction of indirect taxation will make the tax system less progressive because indirect taxes are regressive. This can be seen by the reduction in the ATR differences between Don, Mary and Jane after the introduction of indirect taxes and the fact that the ATR for Don has increased significantly and is almost equal to the marginal tax rate.

11.2 Inflation revisited

Inflation is a popular topic which comes up frequently in the exam. In paper 1 typical questions will relate to causes, consequences or cures and the part (b) will normally require some assessment of the effectiveness of a particular government policy to control inflation, the most likely being monetary policy (interest rates). For paper 2, a diagram showing a cause of inflation is likely and for paper 3 the emphasis is likely to be on how inflation is calculated using a simplified CPI together with identification of problems in accurately measuring inflation and definitions of various inflation related concepts.

You are expected to be able to identify and describe differences between inflation, disinflation and deflation from a set of figures. For example:

Year	CPI
2010	99.2
2011	100
2012	103.1
2013	104
2014	103.6

The table above presents various hypothetical measures of price changes over time according to a Consumer Price Index (CPI). For any such index the base year will always have a value of 100 so 2011 is clearly the base year. From 2010 to 2013 there is inflation as the CPI is increasing. However, from 2012 to 2013 the rate of inflation is falling and this is described as **disinflation**. From 2013 to 2014 the CPI actually falls so now we have **deflation**.

Questions will sometimes be set on deflation and possibly increasingly so as since the pandemic deflation has been quite widespread and not confined to Japan as was previously the case. Deflation is generally seen as bad for an economy because it is usually associated with falling AD and therefore reflects a situation of falling income and output and rising unemployment. There is the possibility of 'good' deflation if the decrease in prices is the result of falling costs of production possibly due to a large fall in the world price of oil and various raw materials which cause the SRAS to shift to the right. IB questions on deflation will normally require an analysis of 'bad' deflation and the analysis that is expected is fairly simple and quite simplified if not simplistic. Diagrammatically you are expected to show deflation as simply a shift in AD to the left or a shift in SRAS to the right, in other words as the opposite of inflation. Despite the possibility of good deflation, questions are likely to focus on the reasons that deflation is considered to be a problem. The scenario that is expected is that deflation causes AD to fall further because consumers delay purchases as they expect prices to fall in the future and thus deflation generates a downward spiral of falling prices and falling AD. Once deflation takes hold in an economy it becomes difficult to combat because monetary policy becomes ineffective as interest rates will already have reached a low minimum level. This problem has been evidenced by Japan which has failed to prevent deflation despite a monetary policy that has produced negative interest rates. In practice, deflation and its causes is a rather complex phenomenon but you are not expected to understand or discuss these complexities for answering questions. The standard simplified scenario outlined above is perfectly acceptable.

For those students who are interested in developing a deeper understanding of deflation and its consequences the following points might be of interest.

Students are often baffled that since inflation is bad why is deflation also bad. Shouldn't the opposite of something that is bad be good? It appears to be counter-intuitive.

The reasons that are given relate to expectations and low consumer and business confidence that are associated with deflation and as mentioned in the typical scenario the expected deferring of spending in anticipation of future price falls that generates a 'self-fulfilling prophecy' of continuous deflation. On one level this all sounds feasible and even rational, but on closer examinations it appears to be an exaggerated oversimplification of actual behavior.

In my opinion, there is confusion between cause and effect in the traditional textbook treatment of deflation. Even if we discount 'good' deflation resulting from falling costs of production, deflation is caused by falling AD. This needs to be emphasised because without a fall in AD there cannot be deflation and it is this fall in AD that is associated with a deep recession that is characterised by high unemployment and low business and consumer confidence.

The expected deferral of consumption that supposedly contributes to the persistence of deflation also requires a more realistic examination. Should we assume that the newly unemployed as a result of the deepening recession will begin to delay buying milk and bread and other daily items because they will be cheaper next month? Clearly this is not the case. The only possible deferred expenditures will be for consumer durables such as cars or furniture. These are items that the newly unemployed would not be buying anyway either now or after a month or a year even if they become cheaper. The demand for these items will have fallen already with the onset of the recession and car dealers will be offering low or zero interest cut price deals for cars anyway. It is the fear of unemployment and unemployment itself that is the problem and the cause of deflation rather than deflation itself.

Would the unemployed actually be better off if in addition to their lack of a job they were faced with rising prices as well?

It is also reasonable to expect that during a deep recession with falling AD many firms will be trying to maintain market shares by cutting prices and as has been evidenced during the recent pandemic, many consumers have switched to online shopping where prices are lower than in high street retail outlets.

It is not deflation that causes low consumer and business confidence but rather high and rising unemployment that is the problem.

11.2.1 Core inflation

Although inflation is measured using a CPI, for policy purposes it is often more appropriate to apply a measure that more closely reflects domestic inflationary pressures. For this reason core or underlying inflation is used because this strips out volatile external components such as energy and food prices. For example, the UK Central Bank has an inflation target of 2% so if inflation is at or above 2% it is expected to intervene with an increase in interest rates in order to achieve the target. However, if CPI inflation is 3% but of this 1.5% is the result of an increase in imported oil and petrol prices, intervention is not required because the underlying rate of 1.5% is within the target.

11.2.2 Producer Price Index (PPI)

This is another alternative and useful measure because it records price changes at the factory gate which reflect changes in firm's costs of production. The PPI acts as a good indicator of future price changes since the CPI follows the PPI after a time lag. Keeping an eye on the PPI allows the Central Bank to be pro-active with its inflation target policy.

11.2.3 Re-assessment of inflation in the light of real-world experience

A series of articles in *The Economist* in October 2019, hinted at an end of inflation and identified a new trend in developed economies over the past decade of low or non-existent inflation and since 2014 a general inability of Central Banks to meet their inflation targets of 2%. Even with interest rates close to, at, or below zero combined with expansionary monetary policies including printing money, inflation remained stubbornly low. Monetarists (such as M. Friedman if he was still alive) would be shocked at the new approaches to monetary policy with QE and more recently the printing of money to finance deficit spending and would have predicted high inflation as a result. In actual fact however, this has not occurred and economies have been more concerned with possible deflation rather than inflation.

This apparent disappearance of inflation is quite an important issue and requires some re-interpretation of the role of monetary policy and expectations for a better understanding of economic relationships between inflation, growth and unemployment. As yet there is no definitive explanation for the change in the inflationary process and it seems likely that a combination of factors are responsible, many of which relate to structural changes that have occurred in developed economies. An analysis of these potential causes is clearly outside the scope of an IB economics course and would involve some complex concepts. It is sufficient for the purposes of a revision guide to simply identify the point that inflation is no longer such a meaningful economic indicator and its relationship with the money supply, unemployment and growth has undergone significant changes. At the time of writing (June 2021) some die-hard monetarists are predicting that the current money printing activities of Central Banks will cause a surge in inflation over the next year and it remains to be seen if this will actually occur.

The question *why has inflation disappeared?* or some variation could be a rather interesting topic for an Extended Essay. There are many possible reasons for the phenomenon and several theories have been advanced, for example:

- online shopping giants such as Amazon have seriously cut prices;
- increased globalisation and trade has stimulated more competition and lower prices as a result;
- increases in container ship size has led to falling transport costs;
- wage growth has been stagnant so growth has not led to increased consumer demand;
- technological innovations have led to increased productivity and more efficient production leading to more competitive prices;
- increases in large scale production have led to lower costs as a result of EOS;
- increases in income distribution inequality means less spending on components of CPI and more spending on goods and services that are not components of CPI such as luxury yachts, diamonds and vintage wines;
- related to the above is the possibility that increased income in the economy is being channeled into equity and asset markets rather than being spent on goods and services which means that share prices are rising rather than prices for goods.

These are just some of the possible explanations and in all probability a combination of factors is responsible though in what proportion is difficult to assess. What is certain is that in the light of these current developments in inflation and deflation a general rethinking of inflation policy and in particular monetary policy is in order and monetarism should finally be removed from mainstream economics and relegated to a topic of economic history. Note that the use of 'should' denotes a normative statement which reflects my personal opinion.

11.3 Fiscal policy revisited

With the ascendancy of the monetarist/neoclassical school since the 1980s and the gradual adoption of SSP in developed economies fiscal policy was relegated to a more secondary role and together with the primacy of inflation control as an objective rather than unemployment countries relied increasingly on monetary policy to regulate AD. In many cases fiscal policy was actually demonised and the EU for example required that members of the Eurozone were obliged to limit any budget deficits to <3% of GDP. The prevailing view was that any budget deficit in excess of this together with a large national debt would be unsustainable and would threaten the stability of the economy.

With the apparent removal of the inflation threat, as discussed in the previous section, and the experience of the financial crisis in 2009 and more recently the Covid-19 pandemic there has been something of a resurrection of Keynesian demand management policies generally and expansionary fiscal stimulus policies specifically. Both of the above mentioned economic crises had the effect of creating deep recessions which traditional monetary policies were unable to combat effectively. It was quickly realised that the necessary boost to AD in order to limit the depth of the recession could only effectively come from a more active expansionary fiscal policy. As a result budget deficit restrictions were lifted and fiscal policy became the main policy initiative with monetary policy playing a supporting complementary role rather than being used as a substitute.

Automatic Stabilisers

It is important to note that there are two elements to fiscal policy. One refers to specific changes in government spending or taxation aimed at influencing AD and is known as **discretionary** fiscal policy. The other consists of automatic changes in government spending and/or taxation that are related to fluctuations in the level of economic activity according to the trade cycle. These operate as automatic stabilisers and limit the extent of trade cycle fluctuations. For example, during the recession phase of the cycle there will be an increase in unemployment and a reduction in consumer spending. This automatically leads to an increase in government spending on unemployment benefits and social welfare payment while simultaneously there will be a decrease in tax revenues from income tax and indirect taxes. Thus a recession will automatically create an expansionary fiscal policy. In contrast, during the recovery phase of the cycle there will be an automatic decrease in government spending on unemployment benefits and welfare payments and an automatic increase in tax revenues as spending increases and more people will be paying income tax. In the past, non-Keynesian economists argued that given this automatic element of fiscal policy there was no need for any discretionary fiscal measures. However, since the pandemic, fiscal stimulus has become the foremost policy initiative.

A Final Bit of Advice

Use this guide in conjunction with other material. It should not be used instead of more detailed textbooks and be aware that certain descriptive topics have been covered only very briefly or not at all. Additional tips and instructions of how best to answer exam questions can be found in the Question and Answer guides published in this series.

You are strongly advised to follow all global events that influence the economy and to keep a record of these so that you can build up a bank of real-world examples to use in the exam. You should start by noting the important economic data that exists for your country and/or the country in which you attend school.

The types of statistics that you should know are:

- Unemployment rate
- Inflation rate
- GDP per capita
- Current account as % of GDP
- Growth rate
- HDI ranking

You should also try to keep track of changes in the above over the duration of your course together with changes in the exchange rate of your country's currency against the dollar, the price of oil and any other factors that are being discussed in the news. Don't forget that you and your families are economic agents and that your behavior constitutes part of consumer demand so what affects you is an aspect of market behavior and you are an important representative of the consumer stakeholder group. Use your own shopping experiences as examples of how the market operates and how firms try to promote their goods and how governments try to influence your decisions and how attempts to nudge you in a particular direction are made.

Notes